To: Barbara
From: Donna
With God's Blessing

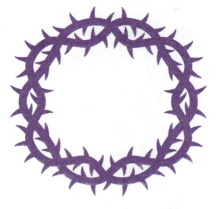

# GOSPEL OF MARK
# JOURNAL

## THE NEW AMERICAN BIBLE

Thomas Nelson Publishers
Nashville

THE REVISED NEW TESTAMENT

NIHIL OBSTAT: Stephen J. Hartdegen, O.F.M., S.S.L.
Censor Deputatus
IMPRIMATUR: †James Cardinal Hickey, S.T.D., J.C.D.
Archbishop of Washington

August 27, 1986

The Gospel of Mark Journal
New American Bible
Copyright © 2001 by Thomas Nelson, Inc.
Scripture texts used in this work are taken from the Revised New Testament of the New American Bible, copyright © 1986 by the Confraternity of Christian Doctrine, Washington, D.C. All rights reserved. No part of the New American Bible may be reproduced or transmitted in any form or by any means, electronic or mechanical, including photocopying, recording, or by any information and retrieval system, without permission in writing from the copyright owner.

Printed in the United States of America
1 2 3 4 5 6—05 04 03 02 01

Thomas Nelson Publishers is pleased to offer the *Gospel of Mark Journal* as an ideal tool for class, group, or individual study, and for personal reflection. Each Bible chapter in this volume is followed by several journaling pages where you may record your thoughts, prayers, and contemplations. Study notes and references related to the various chapters are found at the back of the book.

We trust that you will be enriched spiritually by your time in the Gospel of Mark, and we hope that you will consider expanding your study through the other journals in the series: the *Gospel of Matthew Journal,* the *Gospel of Luke Journal,* and the *Gospel of John Journal.* You may also want to purchase copies for family and friends. These journals make wonderful gifts of invitation to join the journey of faith through the Gospels!

## The Books of the Old Testament and Their Abbreviations

| | | | |
|---|---|---|---|
| Genesis | Gn | Proverbs | Prv |
| Exodus | Ex | Ecclesiastes | Eccl |
| Leviticus | Lv | Song of Songs | Sg |
| Numbers | Nm | Wisdom | Wis |
| Deuteronomy | Dt | Sirach | Sir |
| Joshua | Jos | Isaiah | Is |
| Judges | Jgs | Jeremiah | Jer |
| Ruth | Ru | Lamentations | Lam |
| 1 Samuel | 1 Sm | Baruch | Bar |
| 2 Samuel | 2 Sm | Ezekiel | Ez |
| 1 Kings | 1 Kgs | Daniel | Dn |
| 2 Kings | 2 Kgs | Hosea | Hos |
| 1 Chronicles | 1 Chr | Joel | Jl |
| 2 Chronicles | 2 Chr | Amos | Am |
| Ezra | Ezr | Obadiah | Ob |
| Nehemiah | Neh | Jonah | Jon |
| Tobit | Tb | Micah | Mi |
| Judith | Jdt | Nahum | Na |
| Esther | Est | Habakkuk | Hb |
| 1 Maccabees | 1 Mc | Zephaniah | Zep |
| 2 Maccabees | 2 Mc | Haggai | Hg |
| Job | Jb | Zechariah | Zec |
| Psalms | Ps(s) | Malachi | Mal |

## The Books of the New Testament and Their Abbreviations

| | | | |
|---|---|---|---|
| Matthew | Mt | 1 Timothy | 1 Tm |
| Mark | Mk | 2 Timothy | 2 Tm |
| Luke | Lk | Titus | Ti |
| John | Jn | Philemon | Phlm |
| Acts of the Apostles | Acts | Hebrews | Heb |
| Romans | Rom | James | Jas |
| 1 Corinthians | 1 Cor | 1 Peter | 1 Pt |
| 2 Corinthians | 2 Cor | 2 Peter | 2 Pt |
| Galatians | Gal | 1 John | 1 Jn |
| Ephesians | Eph | 2 John | 2 Jn |
| Philippians | Phil | 3 John | 3 Jn |
| Colossians | Col | Jude | Jude |
| 1 Thessalonians | 1 Thes | Revelation | Rv |
| 2 Thessalonians | 2 Thes | | |

# The Gospel According to Mark

This shortest of all New Testament gospels is likely the first to have been written, yet it often tells of Jesus' ministry in more detail than either Mt or Lk (for example, the miracle stories at 5, 1–20 or 9, 14–29). It recounts what Jesus did in a vivid style, where one incident follows directly upon another. In this almost breathless narrative, Mk stresses Jesus' message about the kingdom of God now breaking into human life as good news (1, 14–15) and Jesus himself as the gospel of God (1, 1; 8, 35; 10, 29). Jesus is the Son whom God has sent to rescue humanity by serving and by sacrificing his life (10, 45).

The opening verse about good news in Mk (1, 1) serves as a title for the entire book. The action begins with the appearance of John the Baptist, a messenger of God attested by scripture. But John points to a mightier one, Jesus, at whose baptism God speaks from heaven, declaring Jesus his Son. The Spirit descends upon Jesus, who eventually, it is promised, will baptize "with the holy Spirit." This presentation of who Jesus really is (1, 1–13) is rounded out with a brief reference to the temptation of Jesus and how Satan's attack fails. Jesus as Son of God will be victorious, a point to be remembered as one reads of Jesus' death and the enigmatic ending to Mark's Gospel.

The key verses at 1, 14–15, which are programmatic, summarize what Jesus proclaims as gospel: fulfillment, the nearness of the kingdom, and therefore the need for repentance and for faith. After the call of the first four disciples, all fishermen (1, 16–20), we see Jesus engaged in teaching (1, 21.22.27), preaching (1, 38–39), and healing (1, 29–31.34.40–45), and exorcising demons (1, 22–27.34.39). The content of Jesus' teaching is only rarely stated, and then chiefly in parables (ch 4) about the kingdom. His cures, especially on the sabbath (3, 1–5); his claim, like God, to forgive sins (2, 3–12); his table fellowship with tax collectors and sinners (2, 14–17); and the statement that his followers need not now fast but should rejoice while Jesus is present (2, 18–22), all stir up opposition that will lead to Jesus' death (3, 6).

In Mk, Jesus is portrayed as immensely popular with the people in Galilee during his ministry (2, 2; 3, 7; 4, 1). He appoints twelve disciples to help preach and drive out demons, just as he does (3, 13–19). He continues to work many miracles; the blocks 4, 35—6, 44 and 6, 45—7, 10 are cycles of stories about healings, miracles at the Sea of Galilee, and marvelous feedings of the crowds. Jesus' teaching in ch 7 exalts the word of God over "the tradition of the elders" and sees defilement as a matter of the heart, not of unclean foods. Yet opposition mounts. Scribes charge that Jesus is possessed by Beelzebul (3, 22). His relatives think him "out of his mind"

(3, 21). Jesus' kinship is with those who do the will of God, in a new eschatological family, not even with mother, brothers, or sisters by blood ties (3, 31–35; cf 6, 1–6). But all too often his own disciples do not understand Jesus (4, 13.40; 6, 52; 8, 17–21). The fate of John the Baptist (6, 17–29) hints ominously at Jesus' own passion (9, 13; cf 8, 31).

A breakthrough seemingly comes with Peter's confession that Jesus is the Christ (Messiah; 8, 27–30). But Jesus himself emphasizes his passion (8, 31; 9, 31; 10, 33–34), not glory in the kingdom (10, 35–45). Momentarily he is glimpsed in his true identity when he is transfigured before three of the disciples (9, 2–8), but by and large Jesus is depicted in Mk as moving obediently along the way to his cross in Jerusalem. Occasionally there are miracles (9, 17–27; 10, 46–52; 11, 12–14.20–21, the only such account in Jerusalem), sometimes teachings (10, 2–11.23–31), but the greatest concern is with discipleship (8, 34—9, 1; 9, 33–50). For the disciples do not grasp the mystery being revealed (9, 32; 10, 32.38). One of them will betray him, Judas (14, 10–11.43–45); one will deny him, Peter (14, 27.31.54.66–72); all eleven men will desert Jesus (14, 27.50).

The passion account, with its condemnation of Jesus by the Sanhedrin (14, 53.55–65; 15, 1a) and sentencing by Pilate (15, 1b–15), is prefaced with the entry into Jerusalem (11, 1–11), ministry and controversies there (11, 15—12, 44), Jesus' Last Supper with the disciples (14, 1–26), and his arrest at Gethsemane (14, 32–52). A chapter of apocalyptic tone about the destruction of the temple (13, 1–2.14–23) and the coming of the Son of Man (13, 24–27), a discourse filled with promises (13, 11.31) and admonitions to be watchful (13, 2.23.37), is significant for Mark's Gospel, for it helps one see that God, in Jesus, will be victorious after the cross and at the end of history.

The Gospel of Mark ends in the most ancient manuscripts with an abrupt scene at Jesus' tomb, which the women find empty (16, 1–8). His own prophecy of 14, 28 is reiterated, that Jesus goes before the disciples into Galilee; "there you will see him." These words may imply resurrection appearances there, or Jesus' parousia there, or the start of Christian mission, or a return to the roots depicted in 1, 9.14–15 in Galilee. Other hands have attached additional endings after 16, 8; see the note on 16, 9–20.

The framework of Mark's Gospel is partly geographical: Galilee (1, 14—9, 49), through the area "across the Jordan" (10, 1) and through Jericho (10, 46–52), to Jerusalem (11, 1—16, 8). Only rarely does Jesus go into Gentile territory (5, 1–20; 7, 24–37), but those who acknowledge him there and the centurion who confesses Jesus at the cross (15, 39) presage the gospel's expansion into the world beyond Palestine.

Mark's Gospel is even more oriented to christology. Jesus is the Son of God (1, 11; 9, 7; 15, 39; cf 1, 1; 14, 61). He is the Messiah, the anointed king of Davidic descent (12, 35; 15, 32), the Greek for which, *Christos*, has, by the time Mark wrote, become in effect a proper name (1, 1; 9, 41). Jesus is also seen as Son of Man, a term used in Mk not simply as a substitute for "I" or for humanity in general (cf 2, 10.27–28; 14, 21) or with reference to a mighty figure who is to come (13, 26; 14, 62), but also in connection with Jesus' predestined, necessary path of suffering and vindication (8, 31; 10, 45).

The unfolding of Mark's story about Jesus is sometimes viewed by interpreters as centered around the term "mystery." The word is employed just once, at 4, 11, in the singular, and its content there is the kingdom, the open secret that God's reign is now breaking into human life with its reversal of human values. There is a related sense in which Jesus' real identity remained a secret during his lifetime, according to Mark, although demons and demoniacs knew it (1, 24; 3, 11; 5, 7); Jesus warned against telling of his mighty deeds and revealing his identity (1, 44; 3, 12; 5, 43; 7, 36; 8, 26.30), an injunction sometimes broken (1, 45; cf 5, 19–20). Further, Jesus teaches by parables, according to Mark, in such a way that those "outside" the kingdom do not understand, but only those to whom the mystery has been granted by God.

Mark thus shares with Paul, as well as with other parts of the New Testament, an emphasis on election (13, 20.22) and upon the gospel as Christ and his cross (cf 1 Cor 1, 23). Yet in Mk the person of Jesus is also depicted with an unaffected naturalness. He reacts to events with authentic human emotion: pity (1, 44), anger (3, 5), triumph (4, 40), sympathy (5, 36; 6, 34), surprise (6, 9), admiration (7, 29; 10, 21), sadness (14, 33–34), and indignation (14, 48–49).

Although the book is anonymous, apart from the ancient heading "According to Mark" in manuscripts, it has traditionally been assigned to John Mark, in whose mother's house (at Jerusalem) Christians assembled (Acts 12, 12). This Mark was a cousin of Barnabas (Col 4, 10) and accompanied Barnabas and Paul on a missionary journey (Acts 12, 25; 13, 3; 15, 36–39). He appears in Pauline letters (2 Tm 4, 11; Phlm 1, 24) and with Peter (1 Pt 5, 13). Papias (ca. A.D. 135) described Mark as Peter's "interpreter," a view found in other patristic writers. Petrine influence should not, however, be exaggerated. The evangelist has put together various oral and possibly written sources—miracle stories, parables, sayings, stories of controversies, and the passion—so as to speak of the crucified Messiah for Mark's own day.

Traditionally, the gospel is said to have been written shortly before A.D. 70 in Rome, at a time of impending persecution and when destruction loomed over Jerusalem. Its audience seems to have been Gentile, unfamiliar with Jewish customs (hence 7, 3–4.11). The book aimed to equip such Christians to stand faithful in the face of persecution (13, 9–13), while going on with the proclamation of the gospel begun in Galilee (13, 10; 14, 9). Modern research often proposes as the author an unknown Hellenistic Jewish Christian, possibly in Syria, and perhaps shortly after the year 70.

The principal divisions of the Gospel according to Mark are the following:

I: The Preparation for the Public Ministry of Jesus (1, 1–13)
II: The Mystery of Jesus (1, 14—8, 26)
III: The Mystery Begins to Be Revealed (8, 27—9, 32)
IV: The Full Revelation of the Mystery (9, 33—16, 8)
  The Longer Ending (16, 9–20)
  The Shorter Ending
  The Freer Logion (in the note on 16, 9–20)

# I: THE PREPARATION FOR THE PUBLIC MINISTRY OF JESUS†

## Chapter 1

¹†The beginning of the gospel of Jesus Christ [the Son of God].

**The Preaching of John the Baptist.**† ²*As it is written in Isaiah the prophet:

> "Behold, I am sending my messenger ahead of you;
> he will prepare your way.
> ³* A voice of one crying out in the desert:
> 'Prepare the way of the Lord,
> make straight his paths.'"

⁴John [the] Baptist appeared in the desert proclaiming a baptism of repentance for the forgiveness of sins. ⁵People of the whole Judean countryside and all the inhabitants of Jerusalem were going out to him and were being baptized by him in the Jordan River as they acknowledged their sins. ⁶†John was clothed in camel's hair, with a leather belt around his waist. He fed on locusts and wild honey. ⁷And this is what he proclaimed: "One mightier than I is coming after me. I am not worthy to stoop and loosen the thongs of his sandals. ⁸*†I have baptized you with water; he will baptize you with the holy Spirit."

**The Baptism of Jesus.** ⁹*It happened in those days that Jesus came from Nazareth of Galilee and was baptized in the Jordan by John. ¹⁰†On coming up out of the water he saw the heavens being torn open and the Spirit, like a dove, descending upon him. ¹¹*And a voice came from the heavens, "You are my beloved Son; with you I am well pleased."

**The Temptation of Jesus.**† ¹²*At once the Spirit drove him out into the desert, ¹³and he remained in the desert for forty days, tempted by Satan. He was among wild beasts, and the angels ministered to him.

## II: THE MYSTERY OF JESUS

**The Beginning of the Galilean Ministry.**† ¹⁴*After John had been arrested, Jesus came to Galilee proclaiming the gospel of God: ¹⁵*"This is the time of fulfillment. The kingdom of God is at hand. Repent, and believe in the gospel."

**The Call of the First Disciples.**† ¹⁶*As he passed by the Sea of Galilee, he saw Simon and his brother Andrew casting their nets into the sea; they were fishermen. ¹⁷Jesus said to them, "Come after me, and I will make you fishers of men." ¹⁸Then they abandoned their nets and followed him. ¹⁹He walked along a little farther and saw James, the son of Zebedee, and his brother John. They too were in a boat mending their nets. ²⁰Then he called them. So they left their father Zebedee in the boat along with the hired men and followed him.

**The Cure of a Demoniac.**† ²¹*Then they came to Capernaum, and on the sabbath he entered the synagogue and taught. ²²*The people were astonished at his teaching, for he taught them as one having authority and not as the scribes. ²³†In their synagogue was a man with an unclean spirit; ²⁴†he cried out, "What have you to do with us, Jesus of Nazareth? Have you come to destroy us? I know who you are—the Holy One of God!" ²⁵Jesus rebuked him and said, "Quiet! Come out of him!" ²⁶The unclean spirit convulsed him and with a loud cry came out of him. ²⁷All were amazed and asked one another, "What is this? A new teaching with authority. He commands even the unclean spirits and they obey him." ²⁸His fame spread everywhere throughout the whole region of Galilee.

**The Cure of Simon's Mother-in-Law.** ²⁹*On leaving the synagogue he entered the house of Simon and Andrew with James and John. ³⁰Simon's mother-in-law lay sick with a fever. They immediately told him about her. ³¹He approached, grasped her hand, and helped her up. Then the fever left her and she waited on them.

**Other Healings.** ³²When it was evening, after sunset, they brought to him all who were ill or possessed by demons. ³³The whole town was gathered at the door. ³⁴He cured many who were sick with various diseases, and he drove out many demons, not permitting them to speak because they knew him.

**Jesus Leaves Capernaum.** ³⁵*Rising very early before dawn, he left and went off to a deserted place, where he prayed. ³⁶Simon and those who were with him pursued him ³⁷and on finding him said, "Everyone is looking for you." ³⁸He told them, "Let us go on to the nearby villages that I may preach there also. For this purpose have I come." ³⁹So he went into their synagogues, preaching and driving out demons throughout the whole of Galilee.

**The Cleansing of a Leper.** ⁴⁰*†A leper came to him [and kneeling down] begged him and said, "If you wish, you can make me clean." ⁴¹*Moved with pity, he stretched out his hand, touched him, and said to him, "I do will it. Be made clean." ⁴²*The leprosy left him immediately, and he was made clean. ⁴³Then, warning him sternly, he dismissed him at once. ⁴⁴*Then he said to him, "See that you tell no one anything, but go, show yourself to the priest and offer for your cleansing what Moses prescribed; that will be proof for them." ⁴⁵The man went away and began to publicize the whole matter. He spread the report abroad so that it was impossible for Jesus to enter a town openly. He remained outside in deserted places, and people kept coming to him from everywhere.

# Chapter 2

The Healing of a Paralytic.† ¹*†When Jesus returned to Capernaum after some days, it became known that he was at home. ²Many gathered together so that there was no longer room for them, not even around the door, and he preached the word to them. ³They came bringing to him a paralytic carried by four men. ⁴Unable to get near Jesus because of the crowd, they opened up the roof above him. After they had broken through, they let down the mat on which the paralytic was lying. ⁵†When Jesus saw their faith, he said to the paralytic, "Child, your sins are forgiven." ⁶†Now some of the scribes were sitting there asking themselves, ⁷*†"Why does this man speak that way? He is blaspheming. Who but God alone can forgive sins?" ⁸Jesus immediately knew in his mind what they were thinking to themselves, so he said, "Why are you thinking such things in your hearts? ⁹Which is easier, to say to the paralytic, 'Your sins are forgiven,' or to say, 'Rise, pick up your mat and walk'? ¹⁰†But that you may know that the Son of Man has authority to forgive sins on earth"— ¹¹he said to the paralytic, "I say to you, rise, pick up your mat, and go home." ¹²He rose, picked up his mat at once, and went away in the sight of everyone. They were all astounded and glorified God, saying, "We have never seen anything like this."

The Call of Levi. ¹³*†Once again he went out along the sea. All the crowd came to him and he taught them. ¹⁴*†As he passed by, he saw Levi, son of Alphaeus, sitting at the customs post. He said to him, "Follow me." And he got up and followed him. ¹⁵†While he was at table in his house, many tax collectors and sinners sat with Jesus and his disciples; for there were many who followed him. ¹⁶†Some scribes who were Pharisees saw that he was eating with sinners and tax collectors and said to his disciples, "Why does he eat with tax collectors and sinners?" ¹⁷†Jesus heard this and said to them [that], "Those who are well do not need a physician, but the sick do. I did not come to call the righteous but sinners."

The Question about Fasting.† ¹⁸*The disciples of John and of the Pharisees were accustomed to fast. People came to him and objected, "Why do the disciples of John and the disciples of the Pharisees fast, but your disciples do not fast?" ¹⁹†Jesus answered them, "Can the wedding guests fast while the bridegroom is with them? As long as they have the bridegroom with them they cannot fast. ²⁰But the days will come when the bridegroom is taken away from them, and then they will fast on that day. ²¹No one sews a piece of unshrunken cloth on an old cloak. If he does, its fullness pulls away, the new from the old, and the tear gets worse. ²²Likewise, no one pours new wine into old wineskins. Otherwise, the wine will burst the skins, and both the wine and the skins are ruined. Rather, new wine is poured into fresh wineskins."

The Disciples and the Sabbath.† ²³*As he was passing through a field of grain on the sabbath, his disciples began to make a path while picking the heads of grain. ²⁴*At this the Pharisees said to him, "Look, why are they doing what is unlawful on the sabbath?" ²⁵†He said to them, "Have you never read what David did when he was in need and he and his companions were hungry? ²⁶*How he went into the house of God when Abiathar was high priest and ate the bread of offering that only the priests could lawfully eat, and shared it with his companions?" ²⁷*†Then he said to them, "The sabbath was made for man, not man for the sabbath. ²⁸†That is why the Son of Man is lord even of the sabbath."

# Chapter 3

**A Man with a Withered Hand.**† ¹*Again he entered the synagogue. There was a man there who had a withered hand. ²They watched him closely to see if he would cure him on the sabbath so that they might accuse him. ³He said to the man with the withered hand, "Come up here before us." ⁴Then he said to them, "Is it lawful to do good on the sabbath rather than to do evil, to save life rather than to destroy it?" But they remained silent. ⁵*Looking around at them with anger and grieved at their hardness of heart, he said to the man, "Stretch out your hand." He stretched it out and his hand was restored. ⁶†The Pharisees went out and immediately took counsel with the Herodians against him to put him to death.

**The Mercy of Jesus.**† ⁷*Jesus withdrew toward the sea with his disciples. A large number of people [followed] from Galilee and from Judea. ⁸Hearing what he was doing, a large number of people came to him also from Jerusalem, from Idumea, from beyond the Jordan, and from the neighborhood of Tyre and Sidon. ⁹He told his disciples to have a boat ready for him because of the crowd, so that they would not crush him. ¹⁰*He had cured many and, as a result, those who had diseases were pressing upon him to touch him. ¹¹*†And whenever unclean spirits saw him they would fall down before him and shout, "You are the Son of God." ¹²He warned them sternly not to make him known.

**The Mission of the Twelve.** ¹³*†He went up the mountain and summoned those whom he wanted and they came to him. ¹⁴*†He appointed twelve [whom he also named apostles] that they might be with him and he might send them forth to preach ¹⁵and to have authority to drive out demons: ¹⁶†[he appointed the twelve:] Simon, whom he named Peter; ¹⁷*James, son of Zebedee, and John the brother of James, whom he named Boanerges, that is, sons of thunder; ¹⁸Andrew, Philip, Bartholomew, Matthew, Thomas, James the son of Alphaeus; Thaddeus, Simon the Cananean, ¹⁹and Judas Iscariot who betrayed him.

**Blasphemy of the Scribes.**† ²⁰*†He came home. Again [the] crowd gathered, making it impossible for them even to eat. ²¹*When his relatives heard of this they set out to seize him, for they said, "He is out of his mind." ²²*†The scribes who had come from Jerusalem said, "He is possessed by Beelzebul," and "By the prince of demons he drives out demons."

**Jesus and Beelzebul.** ²³Summoning them, he began to speak to them in parables, "How can Satan drive out Satan? ²⁴If a kingdom is divided against itself, that kingdom cannot stand. ²⁵And if a house is divided against itself, that house will not be able to stand. ²⁶And if Satan has risen up against himself and is divided, he cannot stand; that is the end of him. ²⁷But no one can enter a strong man's house to plunder his property unless he first ties up the strong man. Then he can plunder his house. ²⁸*Amen, I say to you, all sins and all blasphemies that people utter will be forgiven them. ²⁹†But whoever blasphemes against the holy Spirit will never have forgiveness, but is guilty of an everlasting sin." ³⁰For they had said, "He has an unclean spirit."

**Jesus and His Family.** ³¹*His mother and his brothers arrived. Standing outside they sent word to him and called him. ³²†A crowd seated around him told him, "Your mother and your brothers [and your sisters] are outside asking for you." ³³But he said to them in reply, "Who are my mother and [my] brothers?" ³⁴And looking around at those seated in the circle he said, "Here are my mother and my brothers. ³⁵[For] whoever does the will of God is my brother and sister and mother."

# Chapter 4

The Parable of the Sower.† ¹*†On another occasion he began to teach by the sea. A very large crowd gathered around him so that he got into a boat on the sea and sat down. And the whole crowd was beside the sea on land. ²And he taught them at length in parables, and in the course of his instruction he said to them, ³†"Hear this! A sower went out to sow. ⁴And as he sowed, some seed fell on the path, and the birds came and ate it up. ⁵Other seed fell on rocky ground where it had little soil. It sprang up at once because the soil was not deep. ⁶And when the sun rose, it was scorched and it withered for lack of roots. ⁷Some seed fell among thorns, and the thorns grew up and choked it and it produced no grain. ⁸And some seed fell on rich soil and produced fruit. It came up and grew and yielded thirty, sixty, and a hundredfold." ⁹He added, "Whoever has ears to hear ought to hear."

The Purpose of the Parables. ¹⁰And when he was alone, those present along with the Twelve questioned him about the parables. ¹¹†He answered them, "The mystery of the kingdom of God has been granted to you. But to those outside everything comes in parables, ¹²*so that

> 'they may look and see but not perceive,
>   and hear and listen but not understand,
>   in order that they may not be converted and be forgiven.' "

¹³*†Jesus said to them, "Do you not understand this parable? Then how will you understand any of the parables? ¹⁴The sower sows the word. ¹⁵These are the ones on the path where the word is sown. As soon as they hear, Satan comes at once and takes away the word sown in them. ¹⁶And these are the ones sown on rocky ground who, when they hear the word, receive it at once with joy. ¹⁷But they have no root; they last only for a time. Then when tribulation or persecution comes because of the word, they quickly fall away. ¹⁸Those sown among thorns are another sort. They are the people who hear the word, ¹⁹but worldly anxiety, the lure of riches, and the craving for other things intrude and choke the word, and it bears no fruit. ²⁰But those sown on rich soil are the ones who hear the word and accept it and bear fruit thirty and sixty and a hundredfold."

Parable of the Lamp. ²¹*He said to them, "Is a lamp brought in to be placed under a bushel basket or under a bed, and not to be placed on a lampstand? ²²*For there is nothing hidden except to be made visible; nothing is secret except to come to light. ²³Anyone who has ears to hear ought to hear." ²⁴*He also told them, "Take care what you hear. The measure with which you measure will be measured out to you, and still more will be given to you. ²⁵*To the one who has, more will be given; from the one who has not, even what he has will be taken away."

Seed Grows of Itself.† ²⁶*He said, "This is how it is with the kingdom of God; it is as if a man were to scatter seed on the land ²⁷and would sleep and rise night and day and the seed would sprout and grow, he knows not how. ²⁸Of its own accord the land yields fruit, first the blade, then the ear, then the full grain in the ear. ²⁹And when the grain is ripe, he wields the sickle at once, for the harvest has come."

The Mustard Seed. ³⁰*He said, "To what shall we compare the kingdom of God, or what parable can we use for it? ³¹It is like a mustard seed that, when it is sown in the ground, is the smallest of all the seeds on the earth. ³²†But once it is sown, it springs up and becomes the largest of plants and puts forth large branches, so that the birds of the sky can dwell in its shade." ³³*With many such parables he spoke the word to them as they were able to understand it. ³⁴Without parables he did not speak to them, but to his own disciples he explained everything in private.

The Calming of a Storm at Sea.† ³⁵*On that day, as evening drew on, he said to them, "Let us cross to the other side." ³⁶Leaving the crowd, they took him with them in the boat just as he was. And other boats were with him. ³⁷A violent squall came up and waves were breaking over the boat, so that it was already filling up. ³⁸Jesus was in the stern, asleep on a cushion. They woke him and said to him, "Teacher, do you not care that we are perishing?" ³⁹†He woke up, rebuked the wind, and said to the sea, "Quiet! Be still!" The wind ceased and there was great calm. ⁴⁰Then he asked them, "Why are you terrified? Do you not yet have faith?" ⁴¹*†They were filled with great awe and said to one another, "Who then is this whom even wind and sea obey?"

# Chapter 5

**The Healing of the Gerasene Demoniac.** ¹*†They came to the other side of the sea, to the territory of the Gerasenes. ²†When he got out of the boat, at once a man from the tombs who had an unclean spirit met him. ³The man had been dwelling among the tombs, and no one could restrain him any longer, even with a chain. ⁴In fact, he had frequently been bound with shackles and chains, but the chains had been pulled apart by him and the shackles smashed, and no one was strong enough to subdue him. ⁵Night and day among the tombs and on the hillsides he was always crying out and bruising himself with stones. ⁶Catching sight of Jesus from a distance, he ran up and prostrated himself before him, ⁷†crying out in a loud voice, "What have you to do with me, Jesus, Son of the Most High God? I adjure you by God, do not torment me!" ⁸(He had been saying to him, "Unclean spirit, come out of the man!") ⁹*†He asked him, "What is your name?" He replied, "Legion is my name. There are many of us." ¹⁰And he pleaded earnestly with him not to drive them away from that territory.

¹¹†Now a large herd of swine was feeding there on the hillside. ¹²And they pleaded with him, "Send us into the swine. Let us enter them." ¹³And he let them, and the unclean spirits came out and entered the swine. The herd of about two thousand rushed down a steep bank into the sea, where they were drowned. ¹⁴The swineherds ran away and reported the incident in the town and throughout the countryside. And people came out to see what had happened. ¹⁵As they approached Jesus, they caught sight of the man who had been possessed by Legion, sitting there clothed and in his right mind. And they were seized with fear. ¹⁶Those who witnessed the incident explained to them what had happened to the possessed man and to the swine. ¹⁷Then they began to beg him to leave their district. ¹⁸As he was getting into the boat, the man who had been possessed pleaded to remain with him. ¹⁹†But he would not permit him but told him instead, "Go home to your family and announce to them all that the Lord in his pity has done for you." ²⁰Then the man went off and began to proclaim in the Decapolis what Jesus had done for him; and all were amazed.

**Jairus's Daughter and the Woman with a Hemorrhage.†** ²¹*When Jesus had crossed again [in the boat] to the other side, a large crowd gathered around him, and he stayed close to the sea. ²²*One of the synagogue officials, named Jairus, came forward. Seeing him he fell at his feet ²³†and pleaded earnestly with him, saying, "My daughter is at the point of death. Please, come lay your hands on her that she may get well and live." ²⁴He went off with him, and a large crowd followed him and pressed upon him.

²⁵There was a woman afflicted with hemorrhages for twelve years. ²⁶She had suffered greatly at the hands of many doctors and had spent all that she had. Yet she was not helped but only grew worse. ²⁷She had heard about Jesus and came up behind him in the crowd and touched his cloak. ²⁸†She said, "If I but touch his clothes, I shall be cured." ²⁹Immediately her flow of blood dried up. She felt in her body that she was healed of her affliction. ³⁰Jesus, aware at once that power had gone out from him, turned around in the crowd and asked, "Who has touched my clothes?" ³¹But his disciples said to him, "You see how the crowd is pressing upon you, and yet you ask, 'Who touched me?' " ³²And he looked around to see who had done it. ³³The woman, realizing what had happened to her, approached in fear and trembling. She fell down before Jesus and told him the whole truth. ³⁴*He said to her, "Daughter, your faith has saved you. Go in peace and be cured of your affliction."

³⁵†While he was still speaking, people from the synagogue official's house arrived and said, "Your daughter has died; why trouble the teacher any longer?" ³⁶Disregarding the message that was reported, Jesus said to the synagogue official, "Do not be afraid; just have faith." ³⁷He did not allow anyone to accompany him inside except Peter, James, and John, the brother of James. ³⁸When they arrived at the house of the synagogue official, he caught sight of a commotion, people weeping and wailing loudly. ³⁹*†So he went in and said to them, "Why this commotion and weeping? The child is not dead but asleep." ⁴⁰And they ridiculed him. Then he put them all out. He took along the child's father and mother and those who were with him and entered the room where the child was. ⁴¹†He took the child by the hand and said to her, "[Talitha koum,]" which means, "Little girl, I say to you, arise!" ⁴²The girl, a child of twelve, arose immediately and walked around. [At that] they were utterly astounded. ⁴³He gave strict orders that no one should know this and said that she should be given something to eat.

# Chapter 6

**The Rejection at Nazareth.** ¹*†He departed from there and came to his native place, accompanied by his disciples. ²†When the sabbath came he began to teach in the synagogue, and many who heard him were astonished. They said, "Where did this man get all this? What kind of wisdom has been given him? What mighty deeds are wrought by his hands! ³*†Is he not the carpenter, the son of Mary, and the brother of James and Joses and Judas and Simon? And are not his sisters here with us?" And they took offense at him. ⁴*†Jesus said to them, "A prophet is not without honor except in his native place and among his own kin and in his own house." ⁵†So he was not able to perform any mighty deed there, apart from curing a few sick people by laying his hands on them. ⁶He was amazed at their lack of faith.

**The Mission of the Twelve.** He went around to the villages in the vicinity teaching. ⁷*†He summoned the Twelve and began to send them out two by two and gave them authority over unclean spirits. ⁸†He instructed them to take nothing for the journey but a walking stick—no food, no sack, no money in their belts. ⁹They were, however, to wear sandals but not a second tunic. ¹⁰†He said to them, "Wherever you enter a house, stay there until you leave from there. ¹¹Whatever place does not welcome you or listen to you, leave there and shake the dust off your feet in testimony against them." ¹²So they went off and preached repentance. ¹³*†They drove out many demons, and they anointed with oil many who were sick and cured them.

**Herod's Opinion of Jesus.**† ¹⁴*†King Herod heard about it, for his fame had become widespread, and people were saying, "John the Baptist has been raised from the dead; that is why mighty powers are at work in him." ¹⁵*Others were saying, "He is Elijah"; still others, "He is a prophet like any of the prophets." ¹⁶But when Herod learned of it, he said, "It is John whom I beheaded. He has been raised up."

**The Death of John the Baptist.**† ¹⁷*Herod was the one who had John arrested and bound in prison on account of Herodias, the wife of his brother Philip, whom he had married. ¹⁸*John had said to Herod, "It is not lawful for you to have your brother's wife." ¹⁹†Herodias harbored a grudge against him and wanted to kill him but was unable to do so. ²⁰Herod feared John, knowing him to be a righteous and holy man, and kept him in custody. When he heard him speak he was very much perplexed, yet he liked to listen to him. ²¹She had an opportunity one day when Herod, on his birthday, gave a banquet for his courtiers, his military officers, and the leading men of Galilee. ²²Herodias's own daughter came in and performed a dance that delighted Herod and his guests. The king said to the girl, "Ask of me whatever you wish and I will grant it to you." ²³*He even swore [many things] to her, "I will grant you whatever you ask of me, even to half of my kingdom." ²⁴She went out and said to her mother, "What shall I ask for?" She replied, "The head of John the Baptist." ²⁵The girl hurried back to the king's presence and made her request, "I want you to give me at once on a platter the head of John the Baptist." ²⁶The king was deeply distressed, but because of his oaths and the guests he did not wish to break his word to her. ²⁷*So he promptly dispatched an executioner with orders to bring back his head. He went off and beheaded him in the prison. ²⁸He brought in the head on a platter and gave it to the girl. The girl in turn gave it to her mother. ²⁹When his disciples heard about it, they came and took his body and laid it in a tomb.

The Return of the Twelve. ³⁰*†The apostles gathered together with Jesus and reported all they had done and taught. ³¹*†He said to them, "Come away by yourselves to a deserted place and rest a while." People were coming and going in great numbers, and they had no opportunity even to eat. ³²*So they went off in the boat by themselves to a deserted place. ³³People saw them leaving and many came to know about it. They hastened there on foot from all the towns and arrived at the place before them.

The Feeding of the Five Thousand. ³⁴When he disembarked and saw the vast crowd, his heart was moved with pity for them, for they were like sheep without a shepherd; and he began to teach them many things. ³⁵†By now it was already late and his disciples approached him and said, "This is a deserted place and it is already very late. ³⁶Dismiss them so that they can go to the surrounding farms and villages and buy themselves something to eat." ³⁷He said to them in reply, "Give them some food yourselves." But they said to him, "Are we to buy two hundred days' wages worth of food and give it to them to eat?" ³⁸He asked them, "How many loaves do you have? Go and see." And when they had found out they said, "Five loaves and two fish." ³⁹So he gave orders to have them sit down in groups on the green grass. ⁴⁰†The people took their places in rows by hundreds and by fifties. ⁴¹†Then, taking the five loaves and the two fish and looking up to heaven, he said the blessing, broke the loaves, and gave them to

[his] disciples to set before the people; he also divided the two fish among them all. ⁴²They all ate and were satisfied. ⁴³And they picked up twelve wicker baskets full of fragments and what was left of the fish. ⁴⁴Those who ate [of the loaves] were five thousand men.

The Walking on the Water.† ⁴⁵*†Then he made his disciples get into the boat and precede him to the other side toward Bethsaida, while he dismissed the crowd. ⁴⁶†And when he had taken leave of them, he went off to the mountain to pray. ⁴⁷When it was evening, the boat was far out on the sea and he was alone on shore. ⁴⁸†Then he saw that they were tossed about while rowing, for the wind was against them. About the fourth watch of the night, he came towards them walking on the sea. He meant to pass by them. ⁴⁹But when they saw him walking on the sea, they thought it was a ghost and cried out. ⁵⁰†They had all seen him and were terrified. But at once he spoke with them, "Take courage, it is I, do not be afraid!" ⁵¹He got into the boat with them and the wind died down. They were [completely] astounded. ⁵²*†They had not understood the incident of the loaves. On the contrary, their hearts were hardened.

The Healings at Gennesaret. ⁵³*After making the crossing, they came to land at Gennesaret and tied up there. ⁵⁴As they were leaving the boat, people immediately recognized him. ⁵⁵They scurried about the surrounding country and began to bring in the sick on mats to wherever they heard he was. ⁵⁶*Whatever villages or towns or countryside he entered, they laid the sick in the marketplaces and begged him that they might touch only the tassel on his cloak; and as many as touched it were healed.

# Chapter 7

**The Tradition of the Elders.**† ¹*Now when the Pharisees with some scribes who had come from Jerusalem gathered around him, ²they observed that some of his disciples ate their meals with unclean, that is, unwashed, hands. ³†(For the Pharisees and, in fact, all Jews, do not eat without carefully washing their hands, keeping the tradition of the elders. ⁴And on coming from the marketplace they do not eat without purifying themselves. And there are many other things that they have traditionally observed, the purification of cups and jugs and kettles [and beds].) ⁵†So the Pharisees and scribes questioned him, "Why do your disciples not follow the tradition of the elders but instead eat a meal with unclean hands?" ⁶*He responded, "Well did Isaiah prophesy about you hypocrites, as it is written:

> 'This people honors me with their lips,
>   but their hearts are far from me;
> 7 In vain do they worship me,
>   teaching as doctrines human precepts.'

⁸You disregard God's commandment but cling to human tradition." ⁹He went on to say, "How well you have set aside the commandment of God in order to uphold your tradition! ¹⁰*For Moses said, 'Honor your father and your mother,' and 'Whoever curses father or mother shall die.' ¹¹†Yet you say, 'If a person says to father or mother, "Any support you might have had from me is [qorban]"' (meaning, dedicated to God), ¹²you allow him to do nothing more for his father or mother. ¹³You nullify the word of God in favor of your tradition that you have handed on. And you do many such things." ¹⁴*He summoned the crowd again and said to them, "Hear me, all of you, and understand. ¹⁵Nothing that enters one from outside can defile that person; but the things that come out from within are what defile."[16]†

¹⁷*†When he got home away from the crowd his disciples questioned him about the parable. ¹⁸He said to them, "Are even you likewise without understanding? Do you not realize that everything that goes into a person from outside cannot defile, ¹⁹*†since it enters not the heart but the stomach and passes out into the latrine?" (Thus he declared all foods clean.) ²⁰"But what comes out of a person, that is what defiles. ²¹*From within people, from their hearts, come evil

# Mark 7

thoughts, unchastity, theft, murder, ²²adultery, greed, malice, deceit, licentiousness, envy, blasphemy, arrogance, folly. ²³All these evils come from within and they defile."

**The Syrophoenician Woman's Faith.†** ²⁴*From that place he went off to the district of Tyre. He entered a house and wanted no one to know about it, but he could not escape notice. ²⁵Soon a woman whose daughter had an unclean spirit heard about him. She came and fell at his feet. ²⁶*The woman was a Greek, a Syrophoenician by birth, and she begged him to drive the demon out of her daughter. ²⁷†He said to her, "Let the children be fed first. For it is not right to take the food of the children and throw it to the dogs." ²⁸She replied and said to him, "Lord, even the dogs under the table eat the children's scraps." ²⁹Then he said to her, "For saying this, you may go. The demon has gone out of your daughter." ³⁰When the woman went home, she found the child lying in bed and the demon gone.

**The Healing of a Deaf Man.** ³¹*Again he left the district of Tyre and went by way of Sidon to the Sea of Galilee, into the district of the Decapolis. ³²And people brought to him a deaf man who had a speech impediment and begged him to lay his hand on him. ³³He took him off by himself away from the crowd. He put his finger into the man's ears and, spitting, touched his tongue; ³⁴then he looked up to heaven and groaned, and said to him, "*Ephphatha!*" (that is, "Be opened!") ³⁵And [immediately] the man's ears were opened, his speech impediment was removed, and he spoke plainly. ³⁶†He ordered them not to tell anyone. But the more he ordered them not to, the more they proclaimed it. ³⁷*They were exceedingly astonished and they said, "He has done all things well. He makes the deaf hear and [the] mute speak."

# Chapter 8

**The Feeding of the Four Thousand.†** ¹*In those days when there again was a great crowd without anything to eat, he summoned the disciples and said, ²"My heart is moved with pity for the crowd, because they have been with me now for three days and have nothing to eat. ³If I send them away hungry to their homes, they will collapse on the way, and some of them have come a great distance." ⁴His disciples answered him, "Where can anyone get enough bread to satisfy them here in this deserted place?" ⁵Still he asked them, "How many loaves do you have?" "Seven," they replied. ⁶†He ordered the crowd to sit down on the ground. Then, taking the seven loaves he gave thanks, broke them, and gave them to his disciples to distribute, and they distributed them to the crowd. ⁷They also had a few fish. He said the blessing over them and ordered them distributed also. ⁸They ate and were satisfied. They picked up the fragments left over—seven baskets. ⁹There were about four thousand people.

He dismissed them ¹⁰and got into the boat with his disciples and came to the region of Dalmanutha.

**The Demand for a Sign.†** ¹¹*The Pharisees came forward and began to argue with him, seeking from him a sign from heaven to test him. ¹²He sighed from the depth of his spirit and said, "Why does this generation seek a sign? Amen, I say to you, no sign will be given to this generation." ¹³Then he left them, got into the boat again, and went off to the other shore.

**The Leaven of the Pharisees.** ¹⁴*They had forgotten to bring bread, and they had only one loaf with them in the boat. ¹⁵†He enjoined them, "Watch out, guard against the leaven of the Pharisees and the leaven of Herod." ¹⁶They concluded among themselves that it was because they had no bread. ¹⁷*When he became aware of this he said to them, "Why do you conclude that it is because you have no bread? Do you not yet understand or comprehend? Are your hearts hardened? ¹⁸*Do you have eyes and not see, ears and not hear? And do you not remember, ¹⁹when I broke the five loaves for the five thousand, how many wicker baskets full of fragments you picked up?" They answered him, "Twelve." ²⁰"When I broke the seven loaves for the four thousand, how many full baskets of fragments did you pick up?" They answered [him], "Seven." ²¹He said to them, "Do you still not understand?"

### The Blind Man of Bethsaida.† ²²When they arrived at Bethsaida, they brought to him a blind man and begged him to touch him. ²³*He took the blind man by the hand and led him outside the village. Putting spittle on his eyes he laid his hands on him and asked, "Do you see anything?" ²⁴Looking up he replied, "I see people looking like trees and walking." ²⁵Then he laid hands on his eyes a second time and he saw clearly; his sight was restored and he could see everything distinctly. ²⁶Then he sent him home and said, "Do not even go into the village."

## III: THE MYSTERY BEGINS TO BE REVEALED

### Peter's Confession about Jesus.† ²⁷*Now Jesus and his disciples set out for the villages of Caesarea Philippi. Along the way he asked his disciples, "Who do people say that I am?" ²⁸They said in reply, "John the Baptist, others Elijah, still others one of the prophets." ²⁹And he asked them, "But who do you say that I am?" Peter said to him in reply, "You are the Messiah." ³⁰Then he warned them not to tell anyone about him.

### The First Prediction of the Passion. ³¹*†He began to teach them that the Son of Man must suffer greatly and be rejected by the elders, the chief priests, and the scribes, and be killed, and rise after three days. ³²He spoke this openly. Then Peter took him aside and began to rebuke him. ³³At this he turned around and, looking at his disciples, rebuked Peter and said, "Get behind me, Satan. You are thinking not as God does, but as human beings do."

### The Conditions of Discipleship.† ³⁴*He summoned the crowd with his disciples and said to them, "Whoever wishes to come after me must deny himself, take up his cross, and follow me. ³⁵*†For whoever wishes to save his life will lose it, but whoever loses his life for my sake and that of the gospel will save it. ³⁶What profit is there for one to gain the whole world and forfeit his life? ³⁷What could one give in exchange for his life? ³⁸*Whoever is ashamed of me and of my words in this faithless and sinful generation, the Son of Man will be ashamed of when he comes in his Father's glory with the holy angels."

# Chapter 9

¹*†He also said to them, "Amen, I say to you, there are some standing here who will not taste death until they see that the kingdom of God has come in power."

### The Transfiguration of Jesus.†
²*After six days Jesus took Peter, James, and John and led them up a high mountain apart by themselves. And he was transfigured before them, ³and his clothes became dazzling white, such as no fuller on earth could bleach them. ⁴Then Elijah appeared to them along with Moses, and they were conversing with Jesus. ⁵†Then Peter said to Jesus in reply, "Rabbi, it is good that we are here! Let us make three tents: one for you, one for Moses, and one for Elijah." ⁶He hardly knew what to say, they were so terrified. ⁷†Then a cloud came, casting a shadow over them; then from the cloud came a voice, "This is my beloved Son. Listen to him." ⁸Suddenly, looking around, they no longer saw anyone but Jesus alone with them.

### The Coming of Elijah.†
⁹*As they were coming down from the mountain, he charged them not to relate what they had seen to anyone, except when the Son of Man had risen from the dead. ¹⁰So they kept the matter to themselves, questioning what rising from the dead meant. ¹¹*Then they asked him, "Why do the scribes say that Elijah must come first?" ¹²He told them, "Elijah will indeed come first and restore all things, yet how is it written regarding the Son of Man that he must suffer greatly and be treated with contempt? ¹³*But I tell you that Elijah has come and they did to him whatever they pleased, as it is written of him."

### The Healing of a Boy with a Demon.†
¹⁴*When they came to the disciples, they saw a large crowd around them and scribes arguing with them. ¹⁵Immediately on seeing him, the whole crowd was utterly amazed. They ran up to him and greeted him. ¹⁶He asked them, "What are you arguing about with them?" ¹⁷Someone from the crowd answered him, "Teacher, I have brought to you my son possessed by a mute spirit. ¹⁸Wherever it seizes him, it throws him down; he foams at the mouth, grinds his teeth, and becomes rigid. I asked your disciples to drive it out, but they were unable to do so." ¹⁹He said to them in reply, "O faithless generation, how long will I be with you? How long will I endure you? Bring him to me." ²⁰They brought the boy to him. And when he saw him, the spirit immediately threw

the boy into convulsions. As he fell to the ground, he began to roll around and foam at the mouth. ²¹Then he questioned his father, "How long has this been happening to him?" He replied, "Since childhood. ²²It has often thrown him into fire and into water to kill him. But if you can do anything, have compassion on us and help us." ²³Jesus said to him, " 'If you can!' Everything is possible to one who has faith." ²⁴Then the boy's father cried out, "I do believe, help my unbelief!" ²⁵Jesus, on seeing a crowd rapidly gathering, rebuked the unclean spirit and said to it, "Mute and deaf spirit, I command you: come out of him and never enter him again!" ²⁶Shouting and throwing the boy into convulsions, it came out. He became like a corpse, which caused many to say, "He is dead!" ²⁷But Jesus took him by the hand, raised him, and he stood up. ²⁸When he entered the house, his disciples asked him in private, "Why could we not drive it out?" ²⁹†He said to them, "This kind can only come out through prayer."

The Second Prediction of the Passion. ³⁰*They left from there and began a journey through Galilee, but he did not wish anyone to know about it. ³¹He was teaching his disciples and telling them, "The Son of Man is to be handed over to men and they will kill him, and three days after his death he will rise." ³²But they did not understand the saying, and they were afraid to question him.

## IV: THE FULL REVELATION OF THE MYSTERY

The Greatest in the Kingdom.† ³³*They came to Capernaum and, once inside the house, he began to ask them, "What were you arguing about on the way?" ³⁴But they remained silent. They had been discussing among themselves on the way who was the greatest. ³⁵*Then he sat down, called the Twelve, and said to them, "If anyone wishes to be first, he shall be the last of all and the servant of all." ³⁶Taking a child he placed it in their midst, and putting his arms around it he said to them, ³⁷*"Whoever receives one child such as this in my name, receives me; and whoever receives me, receives not me but the One who sent me."

Another Exorcist.† ³⁸*John said to him, "Teacher, we saw someone driving out demons in your name, and we tried to prevent him because he does not follow us." ³⁹Jesus replied, "Do not prevent him. There is no one who performs a mighty deed in my name who can at the same time speak ill of me. ⁴⁰*For whoever is not against us is for us. ⁴¹*Anyone who gives you a cup of water to drink because you belong to Christ, amen, I say to you, will surely not lose his reward.

Temptations to Sin. ⁴²*"Whoever causes one of these little ones who believe [in me] to sin, it would be better for him if a great millstone were put around his neck and he were thrown into the sea. ⁴³†If your hand causes you to sin, cut it off. It is better for you to enter into life maimed than with two hands to go into Gehenna, into the unquenchable fire.[⁴⁴]† ⁴⁵And if your foot causes you to sin, cut if off. It is better for you to enter into life crippled than with two feet to be thrown into Gehenna.[⁴⁶]† ⁴⁷And if your eye causes you to sin, pluck it out. Better for you to enter into the kingdom of God with one eye than with two eyes to be thrown into Gehenna, ⁴⁸*where 'their worm does not die, and the fire is not quenched.'

The Simile of Salt. ⁴⁹†"Everyone will be salted with fire. ⁵⁰*Salt is good, but if salt becomes insipid, with what will you restore its flavor? Keep salt in yourselves and you will have peace with one another."

# Chapter 10

**Marriage and Divorce.** ¹He set out from there and went into the district of Judea [and] across the Jordan. Again crowds gathered around him and, as was his custom, he again taught them. ²*†The Pharisees approached and asked, "Is it lawful for a husband to divorce his wife?" They were testing him. ³He said to them in reply, "What did Moses command you?" ⁴*They replied, "Moses permitted him to write a bill of divorce and dismiss her." ⁵But Jesus told them, "Because of the hardness of your hearts he wrote you this commandment. ⁶*But from the beginning of creation, 'God made them male and female. ⁷*For this reason a man shall leave his father and mother [and be joined to his wife], ⁸and the two shall become one flesh.' So they are no longer two but one flesh. ⁹Therefore what God has joined together, no human being must separate." ¹⁰In the house the disciples again questioned him about this. ¹¹*He said to them, "Whoever divorces his wife and marries another commits adultery against her; ¹²and if she divorces her husband and marries another, she commits adultery."

**Blessing of the Children.** ¹³*And people were bringing children to him that he might touch them, but the disciples rebuked them. ¹⁴When Jesus saw this he became indignant and said to them, "Let the children come to me; do not prevent them, for the kingdom of God belongs to such as these. ¹⁵*†Amen, I say to you, whoever does not accept the kingdom of God like a child will not enter it." ¹⁶Then he embraced them and blessed them, placing his hands on them.

**The Rich Man.** ¹⁷*As he was setting out on a journey, a man ran up, knelt down before him, and asked him, "Good teacher, what must I do to inherit eternal life?" ¹⁸†Jesus answered him, "Why do you call me good? No one is good but God alone. ¹⁹*You know the commandments: 'You shall not kill; you shall not commit adultery; you shall not steal; you shall not bear false witness; you shall not defraud; honor your father and your mother.' " ²⁰He replied and said to him, "Teacher, all of these I have observed from my youth." ²¹Jesus, looking at him, loved him and said to him, "You are lacking in one thing. Go, sell what you have, and give to [the] poor and you will have treasure in heaven; then come, follow me." ²²At that statement his face fell, and he went away sad, for he had many possessions.

²³*†Jesus looked around and said to his disciples, "How hard it is

for those who have wealth to enter the kingdom of God!" ²⁴The disciples were amazed at his words. So Jesus again said to them in reply, "Children, how hard it is to enter the kingdom of God! ²⁵It is easier for a camel to pass through [the] eye of [a] needle than for one who is rich to enter the kingdom of God." ²⁶They were exceedingly astonished and said among themselves, "Then who can be saved?" ²⁷Jesus looked at them and said, "For human beings it is impossible, but not for God. All things are possible for God." ²⁸Peter began to say to him, "We have given up everything and followed you." ²⁹Jesus said, "Amen, I say to you, there is no one who has given up house or brothers or sisters or mother or father or children or lands for my sake and for the sake of the gospel ³⁰who will not receive a hundred times more now in this present age: houses and brothers and sisters and mothers and children and lands, with persecutions, and eternal life in the age to come. ³¹*But many that are first will be last, and [the] last will be first."

### The Third Prediction of the Passion.

³²*They were on the way, going up to Jerusalem, and Jesus went ahead of them. They were amazed, and those who followed were afraid. Taking the Twelve aside again, he began to tell them what was going to happen to him. ³³"Behold, we are going up to Jerusalem, and the Son of Man will be handed over to the chief priests and the scribes, and they will condemn him to death and hand him over to the Gentiles ³⁴who will mock him, spit upon him, scourge him, and put him to death, but after three days he will rise."

### Ambition of James and John.

³⁵*Then James and John, the sons of Zebedee, came to him and said to him, "Teacher, we want you to do for us whatever we ask of you." ³⁶He replied, "What do you wish [me] to do for you?" ³⁷They answered him, "Grant that in your glory we may sit one at your right and the other at your left." ³⁸*†Jesus said to them, "You do not know what you are asking. Can you drink the cup that I drink or be baptized with the baptism with which I am baptized?" ³⁹They said to him, "We can." Jesus said to them, "The cup that I drink, you will drink, and with the baptism with which I am baptized, you will be baptized; ⁴⁰but to sit at my right or at my left is not mine to give but is for those for whom it has been prepared." ⁴¹When the ten heard this, they became indignant at James and John. ⁴²*†Jesus summoned them and said to them, "You know that those who are recognized as rulers over the Gentiles lord it over them, and their great ones make their authority over them felt. ⁴³But it shall

not be so among you. Rather, whoever wishes to be great among you will be your servant; ⁴⁴whoever wishes to be first among you will be the slave of all. ⁴⁵For the Son of Man did not come to be served but to serve and to give his life as a ransom for many."

### The Blind Bartimaeus.†

⁴⁶*They came to Jericho. And as he was leaving Jericho with his disciples and a sizable crowd, Bartimaeus, a blind man, the son of Timaeus, sat by the roadside begging. ⁴⁷On hearing that it was Jesus of Nazareth, he began to cry out and say, "Jesus, son of David, have pity on me." ⁴⁸And many rebuked him, telling him to be silent. But he kept calling out all the more, "Son of David, have pity on me." ⁴⁹Jesus stopped and said, "Call him." So they called the blind man, saying to him, "Take courage; get up, he is calling you." ⁵⁰He threw aside his cloak, sprang up, and came to Jesus. ⁵¹Jesus said to him in reply, "What do you want me to do for you?" The blind man replied to him, "Master, I want to see." ⁵²Jesus told him, "Go your way; your faith has saved you." Immediately he received his sight and followed him on the way.

# Chapter 11

**The Entry into Jerusalem.**† ¹*When they drew near to Jerusalem, to Bethphage and Bethany at the Mount of Olives, he sent two of his disciples ²and said to them, "Go into the village opposite you, and immediately on entering it, you will find a colt tethered on which no one has ever sat. Untie it and bring it here. ³If anyone should say to you, 'Why are you doing this?' reply, 'The Master has need of it and will send it back here at once.' " ⁴So they went off and found a colt tethered at a gate outside on the street, and they untied it. ⁵Some of the bystanders said to them, "What are you doing, untying the colt?" ⁶They answered them just as Jesus had told them to, and they permitted them to do it. ⁷So they brought the colt to Jesus and put their cloaks over it. And he sat on it. ⁸Many people spread their cloaks on the road, and others spread leafy branches that they had cut from the fields. ⁹*Those preceding him as well as those following kept crying out:

> "Hosanna!
> Blessed is he who comes in the name of the Lord!
> 10  Blessed is the kingdom of our father David that is to come!
> Hosanna in the highest!"

¹¹*He entered Jerusalem and went into the temple area. He looked around at everything and, since it was already late, went out to Bethany with the Twelve.

**Jesus Curses a Fig Tree.**† ¹²*The next day as they were leaving Bethany he was hungry. ¹³Seeing from a distance a fig tree in leaf, he went over to see if he could find anything on it. When he reached it he found nothing but leaves; it was not the time for figs. ¹⁴And he said to it in reply, "May no one ever eat of your fruit again!" And his disciples heard it.

**Cleansing of the Temple.**† ¹⁵*They came to Jerusalem, and on entering the temple area he began to drive out those selling and buying there. He overturned the tables of the money changers and the seats of those who were selling doves. ¹⁶He did not permit anyone to carry anything through the temple area. ¹⁷*Then he taught them saying, "Is it not written:

'My house shall be called a house of prayer for all peoples'? But you have made it a den of thieves."

¹⁸The chief priests and the scribes came to hear of it and were seeking a way to put him to death, yet they feared him because the whole crowd was astonished at his teaching. ¹⁹*When evening came, they went out of the city.

**The Withered Fig Tree.** ²⁰*Early in the morning, as they were walking along, they saw the fig tree withered to its roots. ²¹Peter remembered and said to him, "Rabbi, look! The fig tree that you cursed has withered." ²²Jesus said to them in reply, "Have faith in God. ²³*Amen, I say to you, whoever says to this mountain, 'Be lifted up and thrown into the sea,' and does not doubt in his heart but believes that what he says will happen, it shall be done for him. ²⁴*Therefore I tell you, all that you ask for in prayer, believe that you will receive it and it shall be yours. ²⁵*When you stand to pray, forgive anyone against whom you have a grievance, so that your heavenly Father may in turn forgive you your transgressions.[26]†"

**The Authority of Jesus Questioned.†** ²⁷*They returned once more to Jerusalem. As he was walking in the temple area, the chief priests, the scribes, and the elders approached him ²⁸and said to him, "By what authority are you doing these things? Or who gave you this authority to do them?" ²⁹Jesus said to them, "I shall ask you one question. Answer me, and I will tell you by what authority I do these things. ³⁰Was John's baptism of heavenly or of human origin? Answer me." ³¹They discussed this among themselves and said, "If we say, 'Of heavenly origin,' he will say, '[Then] why did you not believe him?' ³²But shall we say, 'Of human origin'?"—they feared the crowd, for they all thought John really was a prophet. ³³So they said to Jesus in reply, "We do not know." Then Jesus said to them, "Neither shall I tell you by what authority I do these things."

# Chapter 12

**Parable of the Tenants.**† ¹*He began to speak to them in parables. "A man planted a vineyard, put a hedge around it, dug a wine press, and built a tower. Then he leased it to tenant farmers and left on a journey. ²At the proper time he sent a servant to the tenants to obtain from them some of the produce of the vineyard. ³But they seized him, beat him, and sent him away empty-handed. ⁴Again he sent them another servant. And that one they beat over the head and treated shamefully. ⁵He sent yet another whom they killed. So, too, many others; some they beat, others they killed. ⁶He had one other to send, a beloved son. He sent him to them last of all, thinking, 'They will respect my son.' ⁷But those tenants said to one another, 'This is the heir. Come, let us kill him, and the inheritance will be ours.' ⁸So they seized him and killed him, and threw him out of the vineyard. ⁹What [then] will the owner of the vineyard do? He will come, put the tenants to death, and give the vineyard to others. ¹⁰*Have you not read this scripture passage:

> 'The stone that the builders rejected
>   has become the cornerstone;
> 11 by the Lord has this been done,
>   and it is wonderful in our eyes'?"

¹²They were seeking to arrest him, but they feared the crowd, for they realized that he had addressed the parable to them. So they left him and went away.

**Paying Taxes to the Emperor.**† ¹³*†They sent some Pharisees and Herodians to him to ensnare him in his speech. ¹⁴They came and said to him, "Teacher, we know that you are a truthful man and that you are not concerned with anyone's opinion. You do not regard a person's status but teach the way of God in accordance with the truth. Is it lawful to pay the census tax to Caesar or not? Should we pay or should we not pay?" ¹⁵Knowing their hypocrisy he said to them, "Why are you testing me? Bring me a denarius to look at." ¹⁶They brought one to him and he said to them, "Whose image and inscription is this?" They replied to him, "Caesar's." ¹⁷*So Jesus said to them, "Repay to Caesar what belongs to Caesar and to God what belongs to God." They were utterly amazed at him.

**The Question about the Resurrection.**† ¹⁸Some Sadducees, who say there is no resurrection, came to him and put this question to him, ¹⁹*saying, "Teacher, Moses wrote for us, 'If someone's brother dies, leaving a wife but no child, his brother must take the wife and raise up descendants for his brother.' ²⁰Now there were seven brothers. The first married a woman and died, leaving no descendants. ²¹So the second married her and died, leaving no descendants, and the third likewise. ²²And the seven left no descendants. Last of all the woman also died. ²³At the resurrection [when they arise] whose wife will she be? For all seven had been married to her." ²⁴Jesus said to them, "Are you not misled because you do not know the scriptures or the power of God? ²⁵When they rise from the dead, they neither marry nor are given in marriage, but they are like the angels in heaven. ²⁶*As for the dead being raised, have you not read in the Book of Moses, in the passage about the bush, how God told him, 'I am the God of Abraham, [the] God of Isaac, and [the] God of Jacob'? ²⁷He is not God of the dead but of the living. You are greatly misled."

**The Greatest Commandment.**† ²⁸*One of the scribes, when he came forward and heard them disputing and saw how well he had answered them, asked him, "Which is the first of all the commandments?" ²⁹Jesus replied, "The first is this: 'Hear, O Israel! The Lord our God is Lord alone! ³⁰*You shall love the Lord your God with all your heart, with all your soul, with all your mind, and with all your strength.' ³¹*The second is this: 'You shall love your neighbor as yourself.' There is no other commandment greater than these." ³²The scribe said to him, "Well said, teacher. You are right in saying, 'He is One and there is no other than he.' ³³*And 'to love him with all your heart, with all your understanding, with all your strength, and to love your neighbor as yourself' is worth more than all burnt offerings and sacrifices." ³⁴*And when Jesus saw that [he] answered with understanding, he said to him, "You are not far from the kingdom of God." And no one dared to ask him any more questions.

**The Question about David's Son.**† ³⁵*As Jesus was teaching in the temple area he said, "How do the scribes claim that the Messiah is the son of David? ³⁶*David himself, inspired by the holy Spirit, said:

'The Lord said to my lord,
   "Sit at my right hand
      until I place your enemies under your feet." '

37David himself calls him 'lord'; so how is he his son?" [The] great crowd heard this with delight.

**Denunciation of the Scribes.**† 38*In the course of his teaching he said, "Beware of the scribes, who like to go around in long robes and accept greetings in the marketplaces, 39seats of honor in synagogues, and places of honor at banquets. 40They devour the houses of widows and, as a pretext, recite lengthy prayers. They will receive a very severe condemnation."

**The Poor Widow's Contribution.**† 41*He sat down opposite the treasury and observed how the crowd put money into the treasury. Many rich people put in large sums. 42A poor widow also came and put in two small coins worth a few cents. 43Calling his disciples to himself, he said to them, "Amen, I say to you, this poor widow put in more than all the other contributors to the treasury. 44For they have all contributed from their surplus wealth, but she, from her poverty, has contributed all she had, her whole livelihood."

# Chapter 13

The Destruction of the Temple Foretold. † ¹*As he was making his way out of the temple area one of his disciples said to him, "Look, teacher, what stones and what buildings!" ²Jesus said to him, "Do you see these great buildings? There will not be one stone left upon another that will not be thrown down."

The Signs of the End. † ³*As he was sitting on the Mount of Olives opposite the temple area, Peter, James, John, and Andrew asked him privately, ⁴"Tell us, when will this happen, and what sign will there be when all these things are about to come to an end?" ⁵*Jesus began to say to them, "See that no one deceives you. ⁶Many will come in my name saying, 'I am he,' and they will deceive many. ⁷When you hear of wars and reports of wars do not be alarmed; such things must happen, but it will not yet be the end. ⁸Nation will rise against nation and kingdom against kingdom. There will be earthquakes from place to place and there will be famines. These are the beginnings of the labor pains.

The Coming Persecution. ⁹*"Watch out for yourselves. They will hand you over to the courts. You will be beaten in synagogues. You will be arraigned before governors and kings because of me, as a witness before them. ¹⁰†But the gospel must first be preached to all nations. ¹¹*When they lead you away and hand you over, do not worry beforehand about what you are to say. But say whatever will be given to you at that hour. For it will not be you who are speaking but the holy Spirit. ¹²Brother will hand over brother to death, and the father his child; children will rise up against parents and have them put to death. ¹³You will be hated by all because of my name. But the one who perseveres to the end will be saved.

The Great Tribulation. ¹⁴*†"When you see the desolating abomination standing where he should not (let the reader understand), then those in Judea must flee to the mountains, ¹⁵*[and] a person on a housetop must not go down or enter to get anything out of his house, ¹⁶and a person in a field must not return to get his cloak. ¹⁷Woe to pregnant women and nursing mothers in those days. ¹⁸Pray that this does not happen in winter. ¹⁹*For those times will have tribulation such as has not been since the beginning of God's creation until now, nor ever will be. ²⁰If the Lord had not shortened those days, no one would be saved; but for the sake of the elect whom he chose, he did shorten the days. <sup>21</sup>If anyone says to you then, 'Look, here is the Messiah! Look, there he is!' do not believe it. <sup>22</sup>False messiahs and false prophets will arise and will perform signs and wonders in order to mislead, if that were possible, the elect. <sup>23</sup>Be watchful! I have told it all to you beforehand.

**The Coming of the Son of Man.** <sup>24</sup>*"But in those days after that tribulation

> the sun will be darkened,
>  and the moon will not give its light,
> <sup>25</sup> and the stars will be falling from the sky,
>  and the powers in the heavens will be shaken.

<sup>26</sup>*†And then they will see 'the Son of Man coming in the clouds' with great power and glory, <sup>27</sup>and then he will send out the angels and gather [his] elect from the four winds, from the end of the earth to the end of the sky.

**The Lesson of the Fig Tree.** <sup>28</sup>*"Learn a lesson from the fig tree. When its branch becomes tender and sprouts leaves, you know that summer is near. <sup>29</sup>In the same way, when you see these things happening, know that he is near, at the gates. <sup>30</sup>Amen, I say to you, this generation will not pass away until all these things have taken place. <sup>31</sup>Heaven and earth will pass away, but my words will not pass away.

**Need for Watchfulness.** <sup>32</sup>"But of that day or hour, no one knows, neither the angels in heaven, nor the Son, but only the Father. <sup>33</sup>*Be watchful! Be alert! You do not know when the time will come. <sup>34</sup>*It is like a man traveling abroad. He leaves home and places his servants in charge, each with his work, and orders the gatekeeper to be on the watch. <sup>35</sup>Watch, therefore; you do not know when the lord of the house is coming, whether in the evening, or at midnight, or at cockcrow, or in the morning. <sup>36</sup>May he not come suddenly and find you sleeping. <sup>37</sup>What I say to you, I say to all: 'Watch!' "

# Chapter 14

**The Conspiracy against Jesus.**† ¹*†The Passover and the Feast of Unleavened Bread were to take place in two days' time. So the chief priests and the scribes were seeking a way to arrest him by treachery and put him to death. ²They said, "Not during the festival, for fear that there may be a riot among the people."

**The Anointing at Bethany.**† ³*When he was in Bethany reclining at table in the house of Simon the leper, a woman came with an alabaster jar of perfumed oil, costly genuine spikenard. She broke the alabaster jar and poured it on his head. ⁴There were some who were indignant. "Why has there been this waste of perfumed oil? ⁵It could have been sold for more than three hundred days' wages and the money given to the poor." They were infuriated with her. ⁶Jesus said, "Let her alone. Why do you make trouble for her? She has done a good thing for me. ⁷The poor you will always have with you, and whenever you wish you can do good to them, but you will not always have me. ⁸She has done what she could. She has anticipated anointing my body for burial. ⁹Amen, I say to you, wherever the gospel is proclaimed to the whole world, what she has done will be told in memory of her."

**The Betrayal by Judas.** ¹⁰*Then Judas Iscariot, one of the Twelve, went off to the chief priests to hand him over to them. ¹¹When they heard him they were pleased and promised to pay him money. Then he looked for an opportunity to hand him over.

**Preparations for the Passover.** ¹²*†On the first day of the Feast of Unleavened Bread, when they sacrificed the Passover lamb, his disciples said to him, "Where do you want us to go and prepare for you to eat the Passover?" ¹³†He sent two of his disciples and said to them, "Go into the city and a man will meet you, carrying a jar of water. Follow him. ¹⁴Wherever he enters, say to the master of the house, 'The Teacher says, "Where is my guest room where I may eat the Passover with my disciples?"' ¹⁵Then he will show you a large upper room furnished and ready. Make the preparations for us there." ¹⁶The disciples then went off, entered the city, and found it just as he had told them; and they prepared the Passover.

**The Betrayer.** ¹⁷*When it was evening, he came with the Twelve. ¹⁸†And as they reclined at table and were eating, Jesus said, "Amen, I say to you, one of you will betray me, one who is eating with me."

¹⁹They began to be distressed and to say to him, one by one, "Surely it is not I?" ²⁰He said to them, "One of the Twelve, the one who dips with me into the dish. ²¹†For the Son of Man indeed goes, as it is written of him, but woe to that man by whom the Son of Man is betrayed. It would be better for that man if he had never been born."

**The Lord's Supper.**† ²²*While they were eating, he took bread, said the blessing, broke it, and gave it to them, and said, "Take it; this is my body." ²³Then he took a cup, gave thanks, and gave it to them, and they all drank from it. ²⁴†He said to them, "This is my blood of the covenant, which will be shed for many. ²⁵Amen, I say to you, I shall not drink again the fruit of the vine until the day when I drink it new in the kingdom of God." ²⁶*†Then, after singing a hymn, they went out to the Mount of Olives.

**Peter's Denial Foretold.**† ²⁷*Then Jesus said to them, "All of you will have your faith shaken, for it is written:

'I will strike the shepherd,
    and the sheep will be dispersed.'

²⁸But after I have been raised up, I shall go before you to Galilee." ²⁹Peter said to him, "Even though all should have their faith shaken, mine will not be." ³⁰Then Jesus said to him, "Amen, I say to you, this very night before the cock crows twice you will deny me three times." ³¹But he vehemently replied, "Even though I should have to die with you, I will not deny you." And they all spoke similarly.

**The Agony in the Garden.**† ³²*Then they came to a place named Gethsemane, and he said to his disciples, "Sit here while I pray." ³³He took with him Peter, James, and John, and began to be troubled and distressed. ³⁴Then he said to them, "My soul is sorrowful even to death. Remain here and keep watch." ³⁵He advanced a little and fell to the ground and prayed that if it were possible the hour might pass by him; ³⁶†he said, "Abba, Father, all things are possible to you. Take this cup away from me, but not what I will but what you will." ³⁷When he returned he found them asleep. He said to Peter, "Simon, are you asleep? Could you not keep watch for one hour? ³⁸*†Watch and pray that you may not undergo the test. The spirit is willing but the flesh is weak." ³⁹Withdrawing again, he prayed, saying the same thing. ⁴⁰Then he returned once more and found them asleep, for they could not keep their eyes open and did not know what to answer him. ⁴¹He returned a third time and said to them, "Are you still sleeping and taking your rest? It is enough. The hour has come.

Behold, the Son of Man is to be handed over to sinners. ⁴²Get up, let us go. See, my betrayer is at hand."

The Betrayal and Arrest of Jesus. ⁴³*Then, while he was still speaking, Judas, one of the Twelve, arrived, accompanied by a crowd with swords and clubs who had come from the chief priests, the scribes, and the elders. ⁴⁴His betrayer had arranged a signal with them, saying, "The man I shall kiss is the one; arrest him and lead him away securely." ⁴⁵He came and immediately went over to him and said, "Rabbi." And he kissed him. ⁴⁶At this they laid hands on him and arrested him. ⁴⁷One of the bystanders drew his sword, struck the high priest's servant, and cut off his ear. ⁴⁸Jesus said to them in reply, "Have you come out as against a robber, with swords and clubs, to seize me? ⁴⁹Day after day I was with you teaching in the temple area, yet you did not arrest me; but that the scriptures may be fulfilled." ⁵⁰And they all left him and fled. ⁵¹Now a young man followed him wearing nothing but a linen cloth about his body. They seized him, ⁵²but he left the cloth behind and ran off naked.

Jesus before the Sanhedrin. ⁵³*†They led Jesus away to the high priest, and all the chief priests and the elders and the scribes came together. ⁵⁴Peter followed him at a distance into the high priest's courtyard and was seated with the guards, warming himself at the fire. ⁵⁵The chief priests and the entire Sanhedrin kept trying to obtain testimony against Jesus in order to put him to death, but they found none. ⁵⁶Many gave false witness against him, but their testimony did not agree. ⁵⁷†Some took the stand and testified falsely against him, alleging, ⁵⁸*"We heard him say, 'I will destroy this temple made with hands and within three days I will build another not made with hands.' " ⁵⁹Even so their testimony did not agree. ⁶⁰The high priest rose before the assembly and questioned Jesus, saying, "Have you no answer? What are these men testifying against you?" ⁶¹†But he was silent and answered nothing. Again the high priest asked him and said to him, "Are you the Messiah, the son of the Blessed One?" ⁶²*Then Jesus answered, "I am;

> and 'you will see the Son of Man
> seated at the right hand of the Power
> and coming with the clouds of heaven.' "

⁶³At that the high priest tore his garments and said, "What further need have we of witnesses? ⁶⁴You have heard the blasphemy. What do you think?" They all condemned him as deserving to die. ⁶⁵*Some be-

gan to spit on him. They blindfolded him and struck him and said to him, "Prophesy!" And the guards greeted him with blows.

Peter's Denial of Jesus. 66*While Peter was below in the courtyard, one of the high priest's maids came along. 67Seeing Peter warming himself, she looked intently at him and said, "You too were with the Nazarene, Jesus." 68†But he denied it saying, "I neither know nor understand what you are talking about." So he went out into the outer court. [Then the cock crowed.] 69The maid saw him and began again to say to the bystanders, "This man is one of them." 70Once again he denied it. A little later the bystanders said to Peter once more, "Surely you are one of them; for you too are a Galilean." 71He began to curse and to swear, "I do not know this man about whom you are talking." 72*And immediately a cock crowed a second time. Then Peter remembered the word that Jesus had said to him, "Before the cock crows twice you will deny me three times." He broke down and wept.

# Chapter 15

**Jesus before Pilate.** ¹*†As soon as morning came, the chief priests with the elders and the scribes, that is, the whole Sanhedrin, held a council. They bound Jesus, led him away, and handed him over to Pilate. ²†Pilate questioned him, "Are you the king of the Jews?" He said to him in reply, "You say so." ³The chief priests accused him of many things. ⁴Again Pilate questioned him, "Have you no answer? See how many things they accuse you of." ⁵Jesus gave him no further answer, so that Pilate was amazed.

**The Sentence of Death.**† ⁶*Now on the occasion of the feast he used to release to them one prisoner whom they requested. ⁷†A man called Barabbas was then in prison along with the rebels who had committed murder in a rebellion. ⁸The crowd came forward and began to ask him to do for them as he was accustomed. ⁹Pilate answered, "Do you want me to release to you the king of the Jews?" ¹⁰For he knew that it was out of envy that the chief priests had handed him over. ¹¹But the chief priests stirred up the crowd to have him release Barabbas for them instead. ¹²Pilate again said to them in reply, "Then what [do you want] me to do with [the man you call] the king of the Jews?" ¹³†They shouted again, "Crucify him." ¹⁴Pilate said to them, "Why? What evil has he done?" They only shouted the louder, "Crucify him." ¹⁵†So Pilate, wishing to satisfy the crowd, released Barabbas to them and, after he had Jesus scourged, handed him over to be crucified.

**Mockery by the Soldiers.** ¹⁶*†The soldiers led him away inside the palace, that is, the praetorium, and assembled the whole cohort. ¹⁷They clothed him in purple and, weaving a crown of thorns, placed it on him. ¹⁸They began to salute him with, "Hail, King of the Jews!" ¹⁹and kept striking his head with a reed and spitting upon him. They knelt before him in homage. ²⁰And when they had mocked him, they stripped him of the purple cloak, dressed him in his own clothes, and led him out to crucify him.

**The Way of the Cross.** ²¹*†They pressed into service a passer-by, Simon, a Cyrenian, who was coming in from the country, the father of Alexander and Rufus, to carry his cross.

**The Crucifixion.** ²²*They brought him to the place of Golgotha (which is translated Place of the Skull). ²³They gave him wine drugged with myrrh, but he did not take it. ²⁴*†Then they crucified him and divided his garments by casting lots for them to see what each should take. ²⁵†It was nine o'clock in the morning when they crucified him. ²⁶†The inscription of the charge against him read, "The King of the Jews." ²⁷*With him they crucified two revolutionaries, one on his right and one on his left.[28]† ²⁹*†Those passing by reviled him, shaking their heads and saying, "Aha! You who would destroy the temple and rebuild it in three days, ³⁰save yourself by coming down from the cross." ³¹Likewise the chief priests, with the scribes, mocked him among themselves and said, "He saved others; he cannot save himself. ³²*Let the Messiah, the King of Israel, come down now from the cross that we may see and believe." Those who were crucified with him also kept abusing him.

**The Death of Jesus.** ³³At noon darkness came over the whole land until three in the afternoon. ³⁴*†And at three o'clock Jesus cried out in a loud voice, *"Eloi, Eloi, lema sabachthani?"* which is translated, "My God, my God, why have you forsaken me?" ³⁵†Some of the bystanders who heard it said, "Look, he is calling Elijah." ³⁶One of them ran, soaked a sponge with wine, put it on a reed, and gave it to him to drink, saying, "Wait, let us see if Elijah comes to take him down." ³⁷Jesus gave a loud cry and breathed his last. ³⁸†The veil of the sanctuary was torn in two from top to bottom. ³⁹*†When the centurion who stood facing him saw how he breathed his last he said, "Truly this man was the Son of God!" ⁴⁰*†There were also women looking on from a distance. Among them were Mary Magdalene, Mary the mother of the younger James and of Joses, and Salome. ⁴¹These women had followed him when he was in Galilee and ministered to him. There were also many other women who had come up with him to Jerusalem.

**The Burial of Jesus.** ⁴²*When it was already evening, since it was the day of preparation, the day before the sabbath, ⁴³†Joseph of Arimathea, a distinguished member of the council, who was himself awaiting the kingdom of God, came and courageously went to Pilate and asked for the body of Jesus. ⁴⁴Pilate was amazed that he was already dead. He summoned the centurion and asked him if Jesus had already died. ⁴⁵And when he learned of it from the centurion, he gave the body to Joseph. ⁴⁶Having bought a linen cloth, he took him down, wrapped him in the linen cloth and laid him in a tomb that had been hewn out of the rock. Then he rolled a stone against the entrance to the tomb. ⁴⁷Mary Magdalene and Mary the mother of Joses watched where he was laid.

# Chapter 16

**The Resurrection of Jesus.**† ¹*When the sabbath was over, Mary Magdalene, Mary, the mother of James, and Salome bought spices so that they might go and anoint him. ²Very early when the sun had risen, on the first day of the week, they came to the tomb. ³They were saying to one another, "Who will roll back the stone for us from the entrance to the tomb?" ⁴When they looked up, they saw that the stone had been rolled back; it was very large. ⁵*On entering the tomb they saw a young man sitting on the right side, clothed in a white robe, and they were utterly amazed. ⁶He said to them, "Do not be amazed! You seek Jesus of Nazareth, the crucified. He has been raised; he is not here. Behold, the place where they laid him. ⁷*But go and tell his disciples and Peter, 'He is going before you to Galilee; there you will see him, as he told you.' " ⁸Then they went out and fled from the tomb, seized with trembling and bewilderment. They said nothing to anyone, for they were afraid.

## THE LONGER ENDING†

**The Appearance to Mary Magdalene.** [⁹*When he had risen, early on the first day of the week, he appeared first to Mary Magdalene, out of whom he had driven seven demons. ¹⁰*She went and told his companions who were mourning and weeping. ¹¹When they heard that he was alive and had been seen by her, they did not believe.

**The Appearance to Two Disciples.** ¹²*After this he appeared in another form to two of them walking along on their way to the country. ¹³They returned and told the others; but they did not believe them either.

**The Commissioning of the Eleven.** ¹⁴*[But] later, as the eleven were at table, he appeared to them and rebuked them for their unbelief and hardness of heart because they had not believed those who saw him after he had been raised. ¹⁵*He said to them, "Go into the whole world and proclaim the gospel to every creature. ¹⁶Whoever believes and is baptized will be saved; whoever does not believe will be condemned. ¹⁷These signs will accompany those who believe: in my name they will drive out demons, they will speak new languages. ¹⁸*They will pick up serpents [with their hands], and if they drink any deadly thing, it will not harm them. They will lay hands on the sick, and they will recover."

**The Ascension of Jesus.** ¹⁹*So then the Lord Jesus, after he spoke to them, was taken up into heaven and took his seat at the right hand of God. ²⁰*But they went forth and preached everywhere, while the Lord worked with them and confirmed the word through accompanying signs.]

## THE SHORTER ENDING

[And they reported all the instructions briefly to Peter's companions. Afterwards Jesus himself, through them, sent forth from east to west the sacred and imperishable proclamation of eternal salvation. Amen.]

# Notes and References

## References and Footnotes on Mark

### *Chapter One References

| | | | |
|---|---|---|---|
| 1, 2–8: | Mt 3, 1–11; Lk 3, 2–16. | 15: | Mt 3, 2. |
| 2: | Mal 3, 1. | 16–20: | Mt 4, 18–22; Lk 5, 2–11. |
| 3: | Is 40, 3; Jn 1, 23. | 21–28: | Lk 4, 31–37. |
| 8: | Jn 1, 27; Acts 1, 5; 11, 16. | 22: | Mt 7, 28–29. |
| 9–11: | Mt 3, 13–17; Lk 3, 21–23; Jn 1, 32–33. | 29–34: | Mt 8, 14–16; Lk 4, 38–41. |
| | | 35–39: | Lk 4, 42–44. |
| 11: | Ps 2, 7. | 40–44: | Mt 8, 2–4; Lk 5, 12–14. |
| 12–13: | Mt 4, 1–11; Lk 4, 1–13. | 41: | 5, 30. |
| 14–15: | Mt 4, 12–17; Lk 4, 14–15. | 42: | Lk 17, 14. |
| | | 44: | Lv 14, 2–32. |

### †Chapter One Footnotes

**1, 1–13:** The prologue of the Gospel according to Mark begins with the title (1) followed by three events preparatory to Jesus' preaching: (1) the appearance in the Judean wilderness of John, baptizer, preacher of repentance, and precursor of Jesus (2–8); (2) the baptism of Jesus, at which a voice from heaven acknowledges Jesus to be God's Son, and the holy Spirit descends on him (9–11); (3) the temptation of Jesus by Satan (12–13).

**1, 1:** *The gospel of Jesus Christ [the Son of God]:* the "good news" of salvation in and through Jesus, crucified and risen, acknowledged by the Christian community as Messiah (8, 29; 14, 61–62) and Son of God (1, 11; 9, 7; 15, 39), although some important manuscripts here omit *the Son of God.*

**1, 2–3:** Although Mark attributes the prophecy to Isaiah, the text is a combination of Mal 3, 1; Is 40, 3; and Ex 23, 20; cf Mt 11, 10; Lk 7, 27. John's ministry is seen as God's prelude to the saving mission of his Son. *The way of the Lord:* this prophecy of Deutero-Isaiah concerning the end of the Babylonian exile is here applied to the coming of Jesus; John the Baptist is to prepare the way for him.

**1, 6:** *Clothed in camel's hair . . . waist:* the Baptist's garb recalls that of Elijah in 2 Kgs 1, 8. Jesus speaks of the Baptist as Elijah who has already come (9, 11–13; Mt 17, 10–12; cf Mal 3, 23–24; Lk 1, 17).

**1, 8–9:** Through the life-giving baptism with the holy Spirit (8), Jesus will create a new people of God. But first he identifies himself with the people of Israel in submitting to John's baptism of repentance and in bearing on their behalf the burden of God's decisive judgment (9; cf 4). As in the desert of Sinai, so here in the wilderness of Judea, Israel's sonship with God is to be renewed.

**1, 10–11:** *He saw the heavens . . . and the Spirit . . . upon him:* indicating divine intervention in fulfillment of promise. Here the descent of the Spirit on Jesus is meant, anointing him for his ministry; cf Is 11, 2; 42, 1; 61, 1; 63, 9. *A voice . . . with you I am well pleased:* God's acknowledgment of Jesus as his unique Son, the object of his love. His approval of Jesus is the assurance that Jesus will fulfill his messianic mission of salvation.

**1, 12–13:** The same Spirit who descended on Jesus in his baptism now drives him into the desert for forty days. The result is radical confrontation and temptation by Satan who attempts to frustrate the work of God. The presence of wild beasts may indicate the horror and danger of the desert regarded as the abode of demons or may reflect the paradise motif of harmony among all creatures; cf Is 11, 6–9. The presence of ministering angels to sustain Jesus recalls the angel who guided the Israelites in the desert in the first Exodus (14, 19; 23, 20) and the angel who supplied nourishment to Elijah in the wilderness (1 Kgs 19, 5–7). The combined forces of good and evil were present to Jesus in the desert. His sustained obedience brings forth the new Israel of God there where Israel's rebellion had brought death and alienation.

**1, 14–15:** *After John had been arrested:* in the plan of God, Jesus was not to proclaim the good news of salvation prior to the termination of the Baptist's active mission. *Galilee:* in the Marcan account, scene of the major part of Jesus' public ministry before his arrest and condemnation. *The gospel of God:* not only the good news from God but about God at work in Jesus Christ. *This is the time of fulfillment:* i.e., of God's promises. *The kingdom of God . . . repent:* see the note on Mt 3, 2.

**1, 16–20:** These verses narrate the call of the first disciples. See the notes on Mt 4, 18–22 and 4, 20.

**1, 21–45:** The account of a single day's ministry of Jesus on a sabbath in and outside the synagogue of Capernaum (21–31) combines teaching and miracles of exorcism and healing. Mention is not made of the content of the teaching but of the effect of astonishment and alarm on the people. Jesus' teaching with authority, making an absolute claim on the hearer, was in the best tradition of the ancient prophets, not of the scribes. The narrative continues with events that evening (32–34; see the notes on Mt 8, 14–17) and the next day (35–39). The cleansing in vv 40–45 stands as an isolated story.

**1, 23:** *An unclean spirit:* so called because of the spirit's resistance to the holiness of God. The spirit knows and fears the power of Jesus to destroy his influence; cf 32.34; 3, 11; 6, 13.

**1, 24:** *What have you to do with us?:* see the note on Jn 2, 4.

**1, 24–25:** *The Holy One of God:* not a confession but an attempt to ward off Jesus' power, reflecting the notion that use of the precise name of an opposing spirit would guarantee mastery over him. Jesus silenced the cry of the unclean spirit and drove him out of the man.

**1, 40:** *A leper:* for the various forms of skin disease, see Lv 13, 1–50 and the note on Lv 13, 2–4. There are only two instances in the Old Testament in which God is shown to have cured a leper (Nm 12, 10–15 and 2 Kgs 5, 1–14). The law of Moses provided for the ritual purification of a leper. In curing the leper, Jesus assumes that the priests will reinstate the cured man into the religious community. See also the note on Lk 5, 14.

### *Chapter Two References

| | | | |
|---|---|---|---|
| 2, 1–12: | Mt 9, 2–8; Lk 5, 18–26. | 23–28: | Mt 12, 1–8; Lk 6, 1–5. |
| 7: | Is 43, 25. | 24: | Dt 23, 25. |
| 13: | 4, 1. | 26: | 1 Sm 21, 2–7 / Lv 24, 5–9. |
| 14–17: | Mt 9, 9–13; Lk 5, 27–32. | 27: | 2 Mc 5, 19. |
| 18–22: | Mt 9, 14–17; Lk 5, 33–39. | | |

### †Chapter Two Footnotes

**2, 1–3, 6:** This section relates a series of conflicts between Jesus and the scribes and Pharisees in which the growing opposition of the latter leads to their plot to put Jesus to death (3, 6).

**2, 1–2:** *He was at home:* to the crowds that gathered in and outside the house Jesus *preached the word,* i.e., the gospel concerning the nearness of the kingdom and the necessity of repentance and faith (1, 14).

**2, 5:** It was the faith of the paralytic and those who carried him that moved Jesus to heal the sick man. Accounts of other miracles of Jesus reveal more and more his emphasis on faith as the requisite for exercising his healing powers (5, 34; 9, 23–24; 10, 52).

**2, 6:** *Scribes:* trained in oral interpretation of the

written law; in Mark's gospel, adversaries of Jesus, with one exception (12, 28.34).

**2, 7:** *He is blaspheming:* an accusation made here and repeated during the trial of Jesus (14, 60–64).

**2, 10:** *But that you may know that the Son of Man . . . on earth:* although vv 8–9 are addressed to the scribes, the sudden interruption of thought and structure in v 10 seems not addressed to them nor to the paralytic. Moreover, the early public use of the designation "Son of Man" to unbelieving scribes is most unlikely. The most probable explanation is that Mark's insertion of v 10 is a commentary addressed to Christians for whom he recalls this miracle and who already accept in faith that Jesus is Messiah and Son of God.

**2, 13:** *He taught them:* see the note on 1, 21–45.

**2, 14:** *As he passed by:* see the note on 1, 16–20. *Levi, son of Alphaeus:* see the note on Mt 9, 9. *Customs post:* such tax collectors paid a fixed sum for the right to collect customs duties within their districts. Since whatever they could collect above this amount constituted their profit, the abuse of extortion was widespread among them. Hence, Jewish customs officials were regarded as sinners (16), outcasts of society, and disgraced along with their families. *He got up and followed him:* i.e., became a disciple of Jesus.

**2, 15:** *In his house:* cf v 1; Mt 9, 10. Lk 5, 29 clearly calls it Levi's house.

**2, 16–17:** This and the following conflict stories reflect a similar pattern: a statement of fact, a question of protest, and a reply by Jesus.

**2, 17:** *Do not need a physician:* this maxim of Jesus with its implied irony was uttered to silence his adversaries who objected that he ate with *tax collectors and sinners* (16). Because the scribes and Pharisees were self-righteous, they were not capable of responding to Jesus' call to repentance and faith in the gospel.

**2, 18–22:** This conflict over the question of fasting has the same pattern as vv 16–17; see the notes on Mt 9, 15 and 9, 16–17.

**2, 19:** *Can the wedding guests fast?:* the bridal metaphor expresses a new relationship of love between God and his people in the person and mission of Jesus to his disciples. It is the inauguration of the new and joyful messianic time of fulfillment and the passing of the old. Any attempt at assimilating the Pharisaic practice of fasting, or of extending the preparatory discipline of John's disciples beyond the arrival of the bridegroom, would be as futile as sewing *a piece of unshrunken cloth on an old cloak* or pouring *new wine into old wineskins* with the resulting destruction of both cloth and wine (21–22). Fasting is rendered superfluous during the earthly ministry of Jesus; cf v 20.

**2, 23–28:** This conflict regarding the sabbath follows the same pattern as in vv 18–22.

**2, 25–26:** *Have you never read what David did?:* Jesus defends the action of his disciples on the basis of 1 Sm 21, 2–7 in which an exception is made to the regulation of Lv 24, 9 because of the extreme hunger of David and his men. According to 1 Sm, the priest who gave the bread to David was Ahimelech, father of Abiathar.

**2, 27:** *The sabbath was made for man:* a reaffirmation of the divine intent of the sabbath to benefit Israel as contrasted with the restrictive Pharisaic tradition added to the law.

**2, 28:** *The Son of Man is lord even of the sabbath:* Mark's comment on the theological meaning of the incident is to benefit his Christian readers; see the note on 2, 10.

**\*Chapter Three References**

| | |
|---|---|
| 3, 1–6: | Mt 12, 9–14; Lk 6, 6–11. |
| 5: | Lk 14, 4. |
| 7–12: | Mt 4, 23–25; 12, 15; Lk 6, 17–19. |
| 10: | 5, 30. |
| 11: | 1, 34; Lk 4, 41. |
| 13–19: | Mt 10, 1–4; Lk 6, 12–16. |
| 14: | 6, 7. |
| 17: | Mt 16, 18; Jn 1, 42. |
| 20: | 2, 2. |
| 21: | Jn 10, 20. |
| 22–30: | Mt 12, 24–32; Lk 11, 15–22; 12, 10. |
| 28: | Lk 12, 10. |
| 31–35: | Mt 12, 46–50; Lk 8, 19–21. |

**†Chapter Three Footnotes**

**3, 1–5:** Here Jesus is again depicted in conflict with his adversaries over the question of sabbath-day observance. His opponents were already ill disposed toward him because they regarded Jesus as a violator of the sabbath. Jesus' question *Is it lawful to do good on the sabbath rather than to do evil?* places the matter in the broader theological context outside the casuistry of the scribes. The answer is obvious. Jesus heals the man with the withered hand in the sight of all and reduces his opponents to silence; cf Jn 5, 17–18.

**3, 6:** In reporting the plot of the Pharisees and Herodians to put Jesus to death after this series of conflicts in Galilee, Mark uses a pattern that recurs in his account of later controversies in Jerusalem (11, 17–18; 12, 13–17). The help of the Herodians, supporters of Herod Antipas, tetrarch of Galilee and Perea, is needed to take action against Jesus. Both series of conflicts point to their gravity and to the impending passion of Jesus.

**3, 7–19:** This overview of the Galilean ministry manifests the power of Jesus to draw people to himself through his teaching and deeds of power. The crowds of Jews from many regions surround Jesus (7–12). This phenomenon prepares the way for creating a new people of Israel. The choice and mission of the Twelve is the prelude (13–19).

**3, 11–12:** See the note on 1, 24–25.

**3, 13:** *He went up the mountain:* here and elsewhere the mountain is associated with solemn moments and acts in the mission and self-revelation of Jesus (6, 46; 9, 2–8; 13, 3). Jesus acts with authority as he *summoned those whom he wanted and they came to him.*

**3, 14–15:** *He appointed twelve [whom he also named apostles] that they might be with him:* literally "he made," i.e., instituted them as apostles to extend his messianic mission through them (6, 7–13). See the notes on Mt 10, 1 and 10, 2–4.

**3, 16:** *Simon, whom he named Peter:* Mark indicates that Simon's name was changed on this occasion. Peter is first in all lists of the apostles (Mt 10, 2; Lk 6, 14; Acts 1, 13; cf 1 Cor 15, 5–8).

**3, 20–35:** Within the narrative of the coming of Jesus' relatives (20–21) is inserted the account of the unbelieving scribes from Jerusalem who attributed Jesus' power over demons to Beelzebul (22–30); see the note on 5, 21–43. There were those even among the relatives of Jesus who disbelieved and regarded Jesus as *out of his mind* (21). Against this background, Jesus is informed of the arrival of his mother and brothers [and sisters] (32). He responds by showing that not family ties but doing God's will (35) is decisive in the kingdom; cf the note on Mt 12, 46–50.

**3, 20:** *He came home:* cf 2, 1–2 and see the note on 2, 15.

**3, 22:** *By Beelzebul:* see the note on Mt 10, 25. Two accusations are leveled against Jesus: (1) that *he is possessed* by an unclean spirit, and (2) *by the prince of demons he drives out demons.* Jesus answers the second charge by a parable (24–27) and responds to the first charge in vv 28–29.

**3, 29:** *Whoever blasphemes against the holy Spirit:*

## Notes and References

this sin is called *an everlasting sin* because it attributes to Satan, who is the power of evil, what is actually the work of the holy Spirit, namely, victory over the demons.
3, 32: *Your brothers:* see the note on 6, 3.

### *Chapter Four References

| | |
|---|---|
| 4, 1–12: | Mt 13, 1–13; Lk 8, 4–10. |
| 1: | 2, 13; Lk 5, 1. |
| 12: | Is 6, 9; Jn 12, 40; Acts 28, 26; Rom 11, 8. |
| 13–20: | Mt 13, 18–23; Lk 8, 11–15. |
| 21–25: | Lk 8, 16–18. |
| 21: | Mt 5, 15; Lk 11, 33. |
| 22: | Mt 10, 26; Lk 12, 2. |
| 24: | Mt 7, 2; Lk 6, 38. |
| 25: | Mt 13, 12; Lk 19, 26. |
| 26–29: | Jas 5, 7. |
| 30–32: | Mt 13, 31–32; Lk 13, 18–19. |
| 33–34: | Mt 13, 34. |
| 35–40: | Mt 8, 18.23–37; Lk 8, 22–25. |
| 41: | 1, 27. |

### †Chapter Four Footnotes

**4, 1–34:** *In parables* (2): see the note on Mt 13, 3. The use of parables is typical of Jesus' enigmatic method of teaching the crowds (2–9.12) as compared with the interpretation of the parables he gives to his disciples (10–25.33-34), to each group according to its capacity to understand (9–11). The key feature of the parable at hand is the sowing of the seed (3), representing the breakthrough of the kingdom of God into the world. The various types of soil refer to the diversity of response accorded the word of God (4–7). The climax of the parable is the harvest of thirty, sixty, and a hundredfold, indicating the consummation of the kingdom (8). Thus both the present and the future action of God, from the initiation to the fulfillment of the kingdom, is presented through this and other parables (26–29.30-32).

**4, 1:** *By the sea:* the shore of the Sea of Galilee or a boat near the shore (2, 13; 3, 7–8) is the place where Mark depicts Jesus teaching the crowds. By contrast the mountain is the scene of Jesus at prayer (6, 46) or in the process of forming his disciples (3, 13; 9, 2).

**4, 3–8:** See the note on Mt 13, 3–8.

**4, 11–12:** These verses are to be viewed against their background in 3, 6.22 concerning the unbelief and opposition Jesus encountered in his ministry. It is against this background that the distinction in Jesus' method becomes clear of presenting the kingdom to the disbelieving crowd in one manner and to the disciples in another. To the former it is presented in parables and the truth remains hidden; for the latter the parable is interpreted and the mystery is partially revealed because of their faith; see the notes on Mt 13, 11 and 13, 13.

**4, 13–20:** See the note on Mt 13, 18–23.

**4, 26–29:** Only Mark records the parable of the seed's growth. Sower and harvester are the same. The emphasis is on the power of the seed to grow of itself without human intervention (27). Mysteriously it produces *blade* and *ear* and *full grain* (28). Thus the kingdom of God initiated by Jesus in proclaiming the word develops quietly yet powerfully until it is fully established by him at the final judgment (29); cf Rv 14, 15.

**4, 32:** The universality of the kingdom of God is indicated here; cf Ez 17, 23; 31, 6; Dn 4, 17–19.

**4, 35—5, 43:** After the chapter on parables, Mark narrates four miracle stories: 4, 35–41; 5, 1–20; and two joined together in 5, 21–43. See also the notes on Mt 8, 23–34 and 9, 8–26.

**4, 39:** *Quiet! Be still!:* as in the case of silencing a demon (1, 25), Jesus rebukes the wind and subdues the turbulence of the sea by a mere word; see the note on Mt 8, 26.

**4, 41:** Jesus is here depicted as exercising power over wind and sea. In the Christian community this event was seen as a sign of Jesus' saving presence amid persecutions that threatened its existence.

### *Chapter Five References

| | |
|---|---|
| 5, 1–20: | Mt 8, 28–34; Lk 8, 26–39. |
| 9: | Mt 12, 45; Lk 8, 2; 11, 26. |
| 21: | 2, 13. |
| 22–43: | Mt 9, 18–26; Lk 8, 41–56. |
| 34: | Lk 7, 30. |
| 39–40: | Acts 9, 40. |

### †Chapter Five Footnotes

**5, 1:** *The territory of the Gerasenes:* the reference is to pagan territory; cf Is 65, 1. Another reading is "Gadarenes"; see the note on Mt 8, 28.

**5, 2–6:** The man was an outcast from society, dominated by unclean spirits (8.13), living among the tombs. The prostration before Jesus (6) indicates Jesus' power over evil spirits.

**5, 7:** *What have you to do with me?:* cf 1, 24 and see the note on Jn 2, 4.

**5, 9:** *Legion is my name:* the demons were numerous and the condition of the possessed man was extremely serious; cf Mt 12, 45.

**5, 11:** *Herd of swine:* see the note on Mt 8, 30.

**5, 19:** *Go home:* Jesus did not accept the man's request *to remain with him* as a disciple (18), yet invited him to announce to his own people what the Lord had done for him, i.e., proclaim the gospel message to his pagan family; cf 1, 14.39; 3, 14; 13, 10.

**5, 21–43:** The story of the raising to life of Jairus's daughter is divided into two parts: vv 21–24 and 35–43. Between these two separated parts the account of the cure of the hemorrhage victim (25–34) is interposed. This technique of intercalating or sandwiching one story within another occurs several times in Mk: 3, 19b–21 (22–30) 31–35; 6, 6b–13 (14–29) 30; 11, 12–14 (15–19) 20–25; 14, 53 (54) 55–65 (66–73).

**5, 23:** *Lay your hands on her:* this act for the purpose of healing is frequent in Mk (6, 5; 7, 32–35; 8, 23–25; 16, 18) and is also found in Mt 9, 18; Lk 4, 40; 13, 13; Acts 9, 17; 28, 8.

**5, 28:** Both in the case of Jairus and his daughter (23) and in the case of the hemorrhage victim, the inner conviction that physical contact (30) accompanied by faith in Jesus' saving power could effect a cure was rewarded.

**5, 35:** The faith of Jairus was put to a twofold test: (1) that his daughter might be cured and, now that she had died, (2) that she might be restored to life. His faith contrasts with the lack of faith of the crowd.

**5, 39:** *Not dead but asleep:* the New Testament often refers to death as sleep (Mt 27, 52; Jn 11, 11; 1 Cor 15, 6; 1 Thes 4, 13–15); see the note on Mt 9, 24.

**5, 41:** *Arise:* the Greek verb *egeirein* is the verb generally used to express resurrection from death (6, 14.16; Mt 11, 5; Lk 7, 14) and Jesus' own resurrection (16, 6; Mt 28, 6; Lk 24, 6).

## *Chapter Six References

6, 1–6: Mt 13, 54–58; Lk 4, 16–30.
3: 15, 40; Mt 12, 46; Jn 6, 42.
4: Jn 4, 44.
7–11: Mt 10, 1.9–14; Lk 9, 15; 10, 4–11.
13: Jas 5, 14.
14–16: Lk 9, 7–8.
14–29: Mt 14, 1–12.
15: Mt 16, 14.
17: Lk 3, 19–20.
18: Lv 18, 16.
23: Est 5, 3.
27–28: Lk 9, 9.
30: Lk 9, 10.
31: 3, 20; Mt 14, 13; Lk 9, 10.
32–44: Mt 14, 13–21; Lk 9, 10–17; Jn 6, 1–13.
45–51: Mt 14, 22–32; Jn 6, 15–21.
52: 4, 13.
53–56: Mt 14, 34–36.
56: 5, 27–28; Acts 5, 15.

## †Chapter Six Footnotes

**6, 1:** *His native place:* the Greek word *patris* here refers to Nazareth (cf 1, 9; Lk 4, 16.23–24), though it can also mean native land.

**6, 2–6:** See the note on Mt 13, 54–58.

**6, 3:** *Is he not the carpenter?:* no other gospel calls Jesus a carpenter. Some witnesses have "the carpenter's son," as in Mt 13, 55. *Son of Mary:* contrary to Jewish custom, which calls a man the son of his father, this expression may reflect Mark's own faith that God is the Father of Jesus (1, 1.11; 8, 38; 13, 32; 14, 36). *The brother of James . . . Simon:* in Semitic usage, the terms 'brother,' 'sister' are applied not only to children of the same parents, but to nephews, nieces, cousins, half-brothers, and half-sisters; cf Gn 14, 16; 29, 15; Lv 10, 4. While one cannot suppose that the meaning of a Greek word should be sought in the first place from Semitic usage, the Septuagint often translates the Hebrew *ʾāh* by the Greek word *adelphos*, "brother," as in the cited passages, a fact that may argue for a similar breadth of meaning in some New Testament passages. For instance, there is no doubt that in v 17, "brother" is used of Philip, who was actually the half-brother of Herod Antipas. On the other hand, Mark may have understood the terms literally; see also Mt 3, 31–32; 12, 46; 13, 55–56; Lk 8, 19; Jn 7, 3.5. The question of meaning here would not have arisen but for the faith of the church in Mary's perpetual virginity.

**6, 4:** *A prophet is not without honor except . . . in his own house:* a saying that finds parallels in other literatures, especially Jewish and Greek, but without reference to a prophet. Comparing himself to previous Hebrew prophets whom the people rejected, Jesus intimates his own eventual rejection by the nation especially in view of the dishonor his own relatives had shown him (3, 21) and now his townspeople as well.

**6, 5:** *He was not able to perform any mighty deed there:* according to Mark, Jesus' power could not take effect because of a person's lack of faith.

**6, 7–13:** The preparation for the mission of the Twelve is seen in the call (1) of the first disciples to be fishers of men (1, 16–20), (2) then of the Twelve set apart to be with Jesus and to receive authority to preach and expel demons (3, 13–19). Now they are given the specific mission to exercise that authority in word and power as representatives of Jesus during the time of their formation.

**6, 8–9:** In Mk the use of a *walking stick* (8) and *sandals* (9) is permitted, but not in Mt 10, 10 nor in Lk 10, 4. Mark does not mention any prohibition to visit pagan territory and to enter Samaritan towns. These differences indicate a certain adaptation to conditions in and outside of Palestine and suggest in Mark's account a later activity in the church. For the rest, Jesus required of his apostles a total dependence on God for food and shelter; cf vv 35–44; 8, 1–9.

**6, 10–11:** Remaining in the same house as a guest (10) rather than moving to another offering greater comfort avoided any impression of seeking advantage for oneself and prevented dishonor to one's host. Shaking the dust off one's feet served as testimony against those who rejected the call to repentance.

**6, 13:** *Anointed with oil . . . cured them:* a common medicinal remedy, but seen here as a vehicle of divine power for healing.

**6, 14–16:** The various opinions about Jesus anticipate the theme of his identity that reaches its climax in 8, 27–30.

**6, 14:** *King Herod:* see the note on Mt 14, 1.

**6, 17–29:** Similarities are to be noted between Mark's account of the imprisonment and death of John the Baptist in this pericope, and that of the passion of Jesus (15, 1–47). Herod and Pilate, each in turn, acknowledges the holiness of life of one over whom he unjustly exercises the power of condemnation and death (26–27; 15, 9–10.14–15). The hatred of Herodias toward John parallels that of the Jewish leaders toward Jesus. After the deaths of John and of Jesus, well-disposed persons request the bodies of the victims of Herod and of Pilate in turn to give them respectful burial (29; 15, 45–46).

**6, 19:** *Herodias:* see the note on Mt 14, 3.

**6, 30:** *Apostles:* here, and in some manuscripts at 3, 14, Mark calls apostles (i.e., those sent forth) the Twelve whom Jesus sends as his emissaries, empowering them to preach, to expel demons, and to cure the sick (13). Only after Pentecost is the title used in the technical sense.

**6, 31–34:** The withdrawal of Jesus with his disciples to a desert place to rest attracts a great number of people to follow them. Toward this people of the new exodus Jesus is moved with pity; he satisfies their spiritual hunger by teaching them many things, thus gradually showing himself the faithful shepherd of a new Israel; cf Nm 27, 17; Ez 34, 15.

**6, 35–44:** See the note on Mt 14, 13–21. Compare this section with 8, 1–9. The various accounts of the multiplication of loaves and fishes, two each in Mark and in Matthew and one each in Luke and in John, indicate the wide interest of the early church in their eucharistic gatherings; see, e.g., v 41; 8, 6; 14, 22; and recall also the sign of bread in Ex 16; Dt 8, 3–16; Pss 78, 24–25; 105, 40; Wis 16, 20–21.

**6, 40:** *The people . . . in rows by hundreds and by fifties:* reminiscent of the groupings of Israelites encamped in the desert (Ex 18, 21–25) and of the wilderness tradition of the prophets depicting the transformation of the wasteland into pastures where the true shepherd feeds his flock (Ez 34, 25–26) and makes his people beneficiaries of messianic grace.

**6, 41:** On the language of this verse as eucharistic (cf 14, 22), see the notes on Mt 14, 19.20. Jesus observed the Jewish table ritual of blessing God before partaking of food.

**6, 45–52:** See the note on Mt 14, 22–33.

**6, 45:** *To the other side toward Bethsaida:* a village at the northeastern shore of the Sea of Galilee.

**6, 46:** *He went off to the mountain to pray:* see 1, 35–38. In Jn 6, 15 Jesus withdrew to evade any involvement in the false messianic hopes of the multitude.

**6, 48:** *Walking on the sea:* see the notes on Mt 14, 22–33 and on Jn 6, 19.

**6, 50:** *It is I, do not be afraid!:* literally, "I am." This may reflect the divine revelatory formula of Ex 3, 14; Is 41, 4.10.14; 43, 1–3.10.13. Mark implies the hidden identity of Jesus as Son of God.

**6, 52:** *They had not understood . . . the loaves:* the revelatory character of this sign and that of the walking on the sea completely escaped the disciples. *Their hearts were hardened:* in 3, 5–6 hardness of heart was attributed to those who did not accept Jesus and plotted his death. Here the same disposition prevents the disciples from comprehending Jesus' self-revelation through signs; cf 8, 17.

### *Chapter Seven References

- 7, 1–23: Mt 15, 1–20.
- 6: Is 29, 13.
- 10: Ex 21, 17; Lv 20, 9; Dt 5, 16; Eph 6, 2.
- 14–23: Mt 15, 10–20.
- 17: 4, 10.13.
- 19: Acts 10, 15.
- 21: Jer 17, 9.
- 24–30: Mt 15, 21–28.
- 26: Mt 8, 29.
- 31–37: Mt 15, 29–31.
- 37: Mt 15, 31.

### †Chapter Seven Footnotes

**7, 1–23:** See the note on Mt 15, 1–20. Against the Pharisees' narrow, legalistic, and external practices of piety in matters of purification (2–5), external worship (6–7), and observance of commandments, Jesus sets in opposition the true moral intent of the divine law (8–13). But he goes beyond contrasting the law and Pharisaic interpretation of it. The parable of vv 14–15 in effect sets aside the law itself in respect to clean and unclean food. He thereby opens the way for unity between Jew and Gentile in the kingdom of God, intimated by Jesus' departure for pagan territory beyond Galilee. For similar contrast see 2, 1—3, 6; 3, 20–35; 6, 1–6.

**7, 3:** *Carefully washing their hands:* refers to ritual purification.

**7, 5:** *Tradition of the elders:* the body of detailed, unwritten, human laws regarded by the scribes and Pharisees to have the same binding force as that of the Mosaic law; cf Gal 1, 14.

**7, 11:** *Qorban:* a formula for a gift to God, dedicating the offering to the temple, so that the giver might continue to use it for himself but not give it to others, even needy parents.

**7, 16:** Verse 16, "Anyone who has ears to hear ought to hear," is omitted because it is lacking in some of the best Greek manuscripts and was probably transferred here by scribes from 4, (9).23.

**7, 17:** *Away from the crowd . . . the parable:* in this context of privacy the term *parable* refers to something hidden, about to be revealed to the disciples; cf 4, 10–11.34. Jesus sets the Mosaic food laws in the context of the kingdom of God where they are abrogated, and he declares moral defilement the only cause of uncleanness.

**7, 19:** *(Thus he declared all foods clean):* if this bold declaration goes back to Jesus, its force was not realized among Jewish Christians in the early church; cf Acts 10, 1—11, 18.

**7, 24–37:** The withdrawal of Jesus to the district of Tyre may have been for a respite (24), but he soon moved onward to Sidon and, by way of the Sea of Galilee, to the Decapolis. These districts provided a Gentile setting for the extension of his ministry of healing because the people there acknowledged his power (29.37). The actions attributed to Jesus (33–35) were also used by healers of the time.

**7, 27–28:** The figure of a household in which children at table are fed first and then their leftover food is given to the dogs under the table is used effectively to acknowledge the prior claim of the Jews to the ministry of Jesus; however, Jesus accedes to the Gentile woman's plea for the cure of her afflicted daughter because of her faith.

**7, 36:** *The more they proclaimed it:* the same verb *proclaim* attributed here to the crowd in relation to the miracles of Jesus is elsewhere used in Mark for the preaching of the gospel on the part of Jesus, of his disciples, and of the Christian community (1, 14; 13, 10; 14, 9). Implied in the action of the crowd is a recognition of the salvific mission of Jesus; see the note on Mt 11, 5–6.

### *Chapter Eight References

- 8, 1–10: 6, 34–44; Mt 15, 32–39.
- 11–13: Mt 12, 38–39; 16, 1–4.
- 11: Lk 11, 16.
- 14–21: Mt 16, 5–12; Lk 12, 1.
- 17: 4, 13.
- 18: Jer 5, 21; Ez 12, 2.
- 23: 7, 33; Jn 9, 6.
- 27–30: Mt 16, 13–20; Lk 9, 18–21.
- 31–38: Mt 16, 21–27; Lk 9, 22–26.
- 34: Mt 10, 38–39; 16, 24–27; Lk 14, 26–27.
- 35: Jn 12, 25.
- 38: Mt 10, 33; Lk 12, 8.

### †Chapter Eight Footnotes

**8, 1–10:** The two accounts of the multiplication of loaves and fishes (8, 1–10 and 6, 31–44) have eucharistic significance. Their similarity of structure and themes but dissimilarity of detail are considered by many to refer to a single event that, however, developed in two distinct traditions, one Jewish Christian and the other Gentile Christian, since Jesus in Mark's presentation (7, 24–37) has extended his saving mission to the Gentiles.

**8, 6:** See the note on 6, 41.

**8, 11–12:** The objection of the Pharisees that Jesus' miracles are unsatisfactory for proving the arrival of God's kingdom is comparable to the request of the crowd for a sign in Jn 6, 30–31. Jesus' response shows that a sign originating in human demand will not be provided; cf Nm 14, 11.22.

**8, 15:** *The leaven of the Pharisees . . . of Herod:* the corruptive action of leaven (1 Cor 5, 6–8; Gal 5, 9) was an apt symbol of the evil dispositions both of the Pharisees (11–13; 7, 5–13) and of Herod (6, 14–29) toward Jesus. The disciples of Jesus are warned against sharing such rebellious attitudes toward Jesus; cf vv 17, 21.

**8, 22–26:** Jesus' actions and the gradual cure of the blind man probably have the same purpose as in the case of the deaf man (7, 31–37). Some commentators regard the cure as an intended symbol of the gradual enlightenment of the disciples concerning Jesus' messiahship.

**8, 27–30:** This episode is the turning point in Mark's account of Jesus in his public ministry. Popular opinions concur in regarding him as a prophet. The disciples by contrast believe him to be the Messiah. Jesus acknowledges this identification but prohibits them from making his messianic office known to avoid confusing it with ambiguous contemporary ideas on the nature of that office. See further the notes on Mt 16, 13–20.

**8, 31:** *Son of Man:* an enigmatic title. It is used in Dn 7, 13–14 as a symbol of "the saints of the Most High," the faithful Israelites who receive the everlasting kingdom from the Ancient One (God). They are represented by a human figure that contrasts with the various beasts who represent the previous kingdoms of the earth. In the Jewish apocryphal books of 1 Enoch and 4 Ezra the "Son of Man" is not, as in Dn, a group, but a unique figure of extraordinary spiritual endowments, who will be revealed as the one through whom the everlasting kingdom decreed by God will be established. It is possible though doubtful that this individualization of the Son of Man figure had been made in Jesus' time, and therefore his use of the title in that sense is questionable. Of itself, this expression means simply a human being, or, indefinitely, someone, and there are evidences of this use in pre-Christian times. Its use in the New Testament is probably due to Jesus' speaking of himself in that way, "a human being," and the later church's taking this in the sense of the Jewish apocrypha and applying it to him with that meaning. *Rejected by the elders, the chief priests, and the scribes:* the supreme council called the Sanhedrin was made up of seventy-one members of these three groups and presided over by the high priest.

It exercised authority over the Jews in religious matters. See the note on Mt 8, 20.

**8, 34–35:** This utterance of Jesus challenges all believers to authentic discipleship and total commitment to himself through self-renunciation and acceptance of the cross of suffering, even to the sacrifice of life itself. *Whoever wishes to save his life will lose it . . . will save it:* an expression of the ambivalence of life and its contrasting destiny. Life seen as mere self-centered earthly existence and lived in denial of Christ ends in destruction, but when lived in loyalty to Christ, despite earthly death, it arrives at fullness of life.

**8, 35:** *For my sake and that of the gospel:* Mark here, as at 10, 29, equates Jesus with the gospel.

### *Chapter Nine References

| | | | |
|---|---|---|---|
| 9, 1: | Mt 16, 28; Lk 9, 27. | 35: | Mt 20, 27. |
| 2–13: | Mt 17, 1–13; Lk 9, 28–36. | 37: | Mt 10, 40; 18, 5; Jn 13, 20. |
| 9: | 8, 31. | 38–41: | Nm 11, 28; Lk 9, 49–50; 1 Cor 12, 3. |
| 11–12: | Is 53, 3; Mal 3, 23. | 40: | Mt 12, 30. |
| 13: | 1 Kgs 19, 2–10. | 41: | Mt 10, 42; 1 Cor 3, 23. |
| 14–29: | Mt 17, 14–21; Lk 9, 37–43. | 42–47: | Mt 5, 29–30; 18, 6–9; Lk 17, 1–2. |
| 30: | Jn 7, 1. | 48: | Is 66, 24. |
| 30–32: | 8, 31; Mt 17, 22–23; Lk 9, 43–45. | 50: | Lv 2, 13; Mt 5, 13; Lk 14, 34–35; Col 4, 6. |
| 33–37: | Mt 18, 1–5; Lk 9, 46–48. | | |

### †Chapter Nine Footnotes

**9, 1:** *There are some standing . . . come in power:* understood by some to refer to the establishment by God's power of his kingdom on earth and through the church; more likely, as understood by others, a reference to the imminent parousia.

**9, 2–8:** Mk and Mt 17, 1 place the transfiguration of Jesus six days after the first prediction of his passion and death and his instruction to the disciples on the doctrine of the cross; Lk 9, 28 has "about eight days." Thus the transfiguration counterbalances the prediction of the passion by affording certain of the disciples insight into the divine glory that Jesus possessed. His glory will overcome his death and that of his disciples; cf 2 Cor 3, 18; 2 Pt 1, 16–19. The heavenly voice (7) prepares the disciples to understand that in the divine plan Jesus must die ignominiously before his messianic glory is made manifest; cf Lk 24, 25–27. See further the note on Mt 17, 1–8.

**9, 5:** Moses and Elijah represent respectively law and prophecy in the Old Testament and are linked to Mt. Sinai; cf Ex 19, 16—20, 17; 1 Kgs 19, 2.8–14. They now appear with Jesus as witnesses to the fulfillment of the law and the prophets taking place in the person of Jesus as he appears in glory.

**9, 7:** *A cloud came, casting a shadow over them:* even the disciples enter into the mystery of his glorification. In the Old Testament the cloud covered the meeting tent, indicating the Lord's presence in the midst of his people (Ex 40, 34–35) and came to rest upon the temple in Jerusalem at the time of its dedication (1 Kgs 8, 10).

**9, 9–13:** At the transfiguration of Jesus his disciples had seen Elijah. They were perplexed because, according to the rabbinical interpretation of Mal 3, 23–24, Elijah was to come first. Jesus' response shows that Elijah has come, in the person of John the Baptist, to prepare for the day of the Lord. Jesus *must suffer greatly and be treated with contempt* (12) like the Baptist (13); cf 6, 17–29.

**9, 14–29:** The disciples' failure to effect a cure seems to reflect unfavorably on Jesus (14–18.22). In response Jesus exposes their lack of trust in God (19) and scores their lack of prayer (29), i.e., of conscious reliance on God's power when acting in Jesus' name. For Mt, see the note on 17, 14–20. Luke 9, 37–43 centers attention on Jesus' sovereign power.

**9, 29:** *This kind can only come out through prayer:* a variant reading adds "and through fasting."

**9, 33–37:** Mark probably intends this incident and the sayings that follow as commentary on the disciples' lack of understanding (32). Their role in Jesus' work is one of service, especially to the poor and lowly. Children were the symbol Jesus used for the *anawim,* the poor in spirit, the lowly in the Christian community.

**9, 38–41:** Jesus warns against jealousy and intolerance toward others, such as exorcists who do *not follow us.* The saying in v 40 is a broad principle of the divine tolerance. Even the smallest courtesies shown to those who teach in Jesus' name do not go unrewarded.

**9, 43.45.47:** *Gehenna:* see the note on Mt 5, 22.

**9, 44.46:** These verses, lacking in some important early manuscripts, are here omitted as scribal additions. They simply repeat v 48, itself a modified citation of Is 66, 24.

**9, 49:** *Everyone will be salted with fire:* so the better manuscripts. Some add "every sacrifice will be salted with salt." The purifying and preservative use of salt in food (Lv 2, 13) and the refinement effected through fire refer here to comparable effects in the spiritual life of the disciples of Jesus.

### *Chapter Ten References

| | | | |
|---|---|---|---|
| 10, 2–12: | Mt 19, 3–9. | 19: | Ex 20, 12–16; Dt 5, 16–21. |
| 4: | Dt 24, 1–4. | 23: | Prv 11, 28. |
| 6: | Gn 1, 27. | 31: | Mt 19, 30; Lk 13, 30. |
| 7–8: | Gn 2, 24; 1 Cor 6, 16; Eph 5, 31. | 32–34: | 8, 31; Mt 20, 17–19; Lk 18, 31–33. |
| 11–12: | Mt 5, 32; Lk 16, 18; 1 Cor 7, 10–11. | 35–45: | Mt 20, 20–28. |
| 13–16: | Mt 19, 13–15; Lk 18, 15–17. | 38: | Lk 12, 50. |
| 13: | Lk 9, 47. | 42–45: | Lk 22, 25–27. |
| 15: | Mt 18, 3. | 46–52: | Mt 20, 29–34; Lk 18, 35–43. |
| 17–31: | Mt 19, 16–30; Lk 18, 18–30. | | |

### †Chapter Ten Footnotes

**10, 2–9:** In the dialogue between Jesus and the Pharisees on the subject of divorce, Jesus declares that the law of Moses permitted divorce (Dt 24, 1) only *because of the hardness of your hearts* (4–5). In citing Gn 1, 27 and 2, 24, Jesus proclaims permanence to be the divine intent from the beginning concerning human marriage (6–8). He reaffirms this with the declaration that *what God has joined together, no human being must separate* (9). See further the notes on Mt 5, 31–32 and 19, 3–9.

**10, 15:** *Whoever does not accept the kingdom of God like a child:* i.e., in total dependence upon and obedience to the gospel; cf Mt 18, 3–4.

**10, 18:** *Why do you call me good?:* Jesus repudiates the term "good" for himself and directs it to God, the source of all goodness who alone can grant the gift of eternal life; cf Mt 19, 16–17.

**10, 23–27:** In the Old Testament wealth and material goods are considered a sign of God's favor (Jb 1, 10; Ps 128, 1–2; Is 3, 10). The words of Jesus in 23–25 provoke astonishment among the disciples because of their apparent contradiction of the Old Testament concept (24.26). Since wealth, power, and merit generate false security, Jesus rejects them utterly as a claim to enter the kingdom. Achievement of salvation is beyond human capability and depends solely on the goodness of God who offers it as a gift (27).

**10, 38–40:** *Can you drink the cup . . . I am baptized?:* the metaphor of drinking the cup is used in the Old Testament to refer to acceptance of the destiny assigned by God; see the note on Ps 11, 6. In Jesus' case, this involves divine judgment on sin that Jesus the innocent one is to expiate on behalf of the guilty (14, 24; Is 53, 5). His baptism is to be his crucifixion and death for the salvation of the human race; cf Lk 12, 50. The request of James and John for a share in the glory (35–37) must of necessity involve a share in Jesus' sufferings, the endurance of tribulation and suffering for the gospel (39). The authority of assigning places of honor in the kingdom is reserved to God (40).

**10, 42–45:** Whatever authority is to be exercised by the disciples must, like that of Jesus, be rendered as service to others (45) rather than for personal aggrandizement (42–44). The service of Jesus is his passion and death for the sins of the human race (45); cf 14, 24; Is 53, 11–12; Mt 26, 28; Lk 22, 19–20.

**10, 46–52:** See the notes on Mt 9, 27–31 and 20, 29–34.

\*Chapter Eleven References

| | | | |
|---|---|---|---|
| 11, 1–10: | Mt 21, 1–9; Lk 19, 29–38; Jn 12, 12–15. | 17: | Is 56, 7; Jer 7, 11. |
| 9–10: | 2 Sm 7, 16; Ps 118, 26. | 19: | Lk 21, 37. |
| | | 20–24: | Mt 21, 20–22. |
| 11: | Mt 21, 10.17. | 23: | Mt 17, 20–21; Lk 17, 6. |
| 12–14: | Mt 21, 18–20; Lk 13, 6–9. | 24: | Mt 7, 7; Jn 11, 22; 14, 13. |
| 15–18: | Mt 21, 12–13; Lk 19, 45–46; Jn 2, 14–16. | 25: | Mt 6, 14; 18, 35. |
| | | 27–33: | Mt 21, 23–27; Lk 20, 1–8. |

†Chapter Eleven Footnotes

**11, 1–11:** In Mark's account Jesus takes the initiative in ordering the preparation for his entry into Jerusalem (1–6) even as he later orders the preparation of his last Passover Supper (14, 12–16). In vv 9–10 the greeting Jesus receives stops short of proclaiming him Messiah. He is greeted rather as the prophet of the coming messianic kingdom. Contrast Mt 21, 9.

**11, 12–14:** Jesus' search for fruit on the fig tree recalls the prophets' earlier use of this image to designate Israel; cf Jer 8, 13; 29, 17; Jl 1, 7; Hos 9, 10.16. Cursing the fig tree is a parable in action representing Jesus' judgment (20) on barren Israel and the fate of Jerusalem for failing to receive his teaching; cf Is 34, 4; Hos 2, 14; Lk 13, 6–9.

**11, 15–19:** See the note on Mt 21, 12–17.

**11, 26:** This verse, which reads, "But if you do not forgive, neither will your heavenly Father forgive your transgressions," is omitted in the best manuscripts. It was probably added by copyists under the influence of Mt 6, 15.

**11, 27–33:** The mounting hostility toward Jesus came from the chief priests, the scribes, and the elders (27); the Herodians and the Pharisees (12, 13); and the Sadducees (12, 18). By their rejection of God's messengers, John the Baptist and Jesus, their incurred the divine judgment implied in vv 27–33 and confirmed in the parable of the vineyard tenants (12, 1–12).

\*Chapter Twelve References

| | | | |
|---|---|---|---|
| 12, 1–12: | Mt 21, 33–46; Lk 20, 9–19. | 31: | Lv 19, 18; Rom 13, 9; Gal 5, 14; Jas 2, 8. |
| 1: | Is 5, 1–7; Jer 2, 21. | 33: | Dt 6, 4; Ps 40, 7–9. |
| 10–11: | Ps 118, 22–23; Is 28, 16. | 34: | Mt 22, 46; Lk 20, 40. |
| 13–27: | Mt 22, 15–33; Lk 20, 20–39. | 35–37: | Mt 22, 41–45; Lk 20, 41–44. |
| 13: | 3, 6. | 36: | Ps 110, 1. |
| 17: | Rom 13, 7. | 38–40: | Mt 23, 1–7; Lk 11, 43; 20, 45–47. |
| 19: | Dt 25, 5. | | |
| 26: | Ex 3, 6. | | |
| 28–34: | Mt 22, 34–40; Lk 10, 25–28. | 41–44: | Lk 21, 1–4. |
| 30: | Dt 6, 4–5. | | |

†Chapter Twelve Footnotes

**12, 1–12:** The vineyard denotes Israel (Is 5, 1–7). The tenant farmers are the religious leaders of Israel. God is the owner of the vineyard. His servants are his messengers, the prophets. The beloved son is Jesus (1, 11; 9, 7; Mt 3, 17; 17, 5; Lk 3, 22; 9, 35). The punishment of the tenants refers to the religious leaders, and the transfer of the vineyard to others refers to the people of the new Israel.

**12, 13–34:** In the ensuing conflicts (cf also 2, 1—3, 6) Jesus vanquishes his adversaries by his responses to their questions and reduces them to silence (34).

**12, 13–17:** See the note on Mt 22, 15–22.

**12, 18–27:** See the note on Mt 22, 23–33.

**12, 28–34:** See the note on Mt 22, 34–40.

**12, 35–37:** Jesus questions the claim of the scribes about the Davidic descent of the Messiah, not to deny it (Mt 1, 1; Acts 2, 20.34; Rom 1, 3; 2 Tm 2, 8) but to imply that he is more than this. His superiority derives from his transcendent origin, to which David himself attested when he spoke of the Messiah with the name "Lord" (Ps 110, 1). See also the note on Mt 22, 41–46.

**12, 38–40:** See the notes on 7, 1–23 and Mt 23, 1–39.

**12, 41–44:** See the note on Lk 21, 1–4.

\*Chapter Thirteen References

| | | | |
|---|---|---|---|
| 13, 1–2: | Mt 24, 1–2; Lk 21, 5–6. | 15: | Lk 17, 31. |
| | | 19: | Dn 12, 1. |
| 3–8: | Mt 24, 3–8; Lk 21, 7–11. | 24–27: | Mt 24, 29–31; Lk 21, 25–27. |
| 5: | Eph 5, 6; 2 Thes 2, 3. | 24: | Is 13, 10; Ez 32, 7; Jl 2, 10. |
| 9–13: | Mt 24, 9–14; Lk 21, 12–19. | 26: | 14, 62; Dn 7, 13–14. |
| 11–12: | Mt 10, 19–22; Lk 12, 11–12. | 28–32: | Mt 24, 32–36; Lk 21, 29–33. |
| 14–23: | Mt 24, 15–22; Lk 21, 20–24. | 33–37: | Mt 24, 42; 25, 13–15. |
| 14: | Dn 9, 27; Mt 24, 15. | 34: | Mt 25, 14–30; Lk 19, 12–27. |

†Chapter Thirteen Footnotes

**13, 1–2:** The reconstructed temple with its precincts, begun under Herod the Great ca. 20 B.C., was completed only some seven years before it was destroyed by fire in A.D. 70 at the hands of the Romans; cf Jer 26, 18; Mt 24, 1–2. For the dating of the reconstruction of the temple, see further the note on Jn 2, 20.

**13, 3–37:** Jesus' prediction of the destruction of the temple (2) provoked questions that the four named disciples put to him in private regarding the time and the sign *when all these things are about to come to an end* (3–4). The response to their questions was Jesus' eschatological discourse prior to his imminent death. It contained instruction and consolation exhorting the disciples and the church to faith and obedience through the trials that would confront them (5–13). The sign is the presence of *the desolating abomination* (14; see Dn 9, 27), i.e., of the Roman power profaning the temple. Flight from Jerusalem is urged rather than defense of the city through misguided messianic hope (14–23). Intervention will occur only after destruction (24–27), which will happen before the end of the first Christian generation (28–31). No one but the Father knows the precise time, or that of the parousia (32); hence the necessity of constant vigilance (33–37). Luke sets the parousia at a later date, after "the time of the Gentiles" (Lk 21, 24). See also the notes on Mt 24, 1—25, 46.

**13, 10:** *The gospel . . . to all nations:* the period of the Christian mission.

**13, 14:** The participle *standing* is masculine, in contrast to the neuter at Mt 24, 15.

**13, 26:** *Son of Man . . . with great power and glory:* Jesus cites this text from Dn 7, 13 in his response to the high priest, *Are you the Messiah?* (14, 61). In Ex 34, 5; Lv 16, 2; and Nm 11, 25 the clouds indicate the presence of the divinity. Thus in his role of Son of Man, Jesus is a heavenly being who will come in power and glory.

### *Chapter Fourteen References

| | |
|---|---|
| 14, 1–2: | Mt 26, 2–5; Lk 22, 1–2; Jn 11, 45–53. |
| 3–9: | Mt 26, 6–13; Jn 12, 1–8. |
| 10–11: | Mt 26, 14–16; Lk 22, 3–6. |
| 12–16: | Mt 26, 17–19; Lk 22, 7–13. |
| 17–21: | Mt 26, 20–24; Lk 22, 21–23; Jn 13, 21–26. |
| 22–25: | Mt 26, 26–30; Lk 22, 19–20; 1 Cor 11, 23–25. |
| 26–31: | Mt 26, 30–35; Lk 22, 34.39; Jn 13, 36–38. |
| 27: | Zec 13, 7; Jn 16, 32. |
| 32–42: | Mt 26, 36–46; Lk 22, 40–46. |
| 32: | Jn 18, 1. |
| 38: | Rom 7, 5. |
| 43–50: | Mt 26, 47–56; Lk 22, 47–53; Jn 18, 3–11. |
| 53–65: | Mt 26, 57–68; Lk 22, 54–55.63–65.67–71; Jn 18, 12–13. |
| 58: | 15, 29; 2 Cor 5, 1. |
| 62: | 13, 26; Ps 110, 1; Dn 7, 13; Mt 24, 30. |
| 65: | Lk 22, 63–65. |
| 66–72: | Mt 26, 69–75; Lk 22, 56–62; Jn 18, 16–18.25–27. |
| 72: | Jn 13, 38. |

### †Chapter Fourteen Footnotes

**14, 1—16, 8:** In the movement of Mark's gospel the cross is depicted as Jesus' way to glory in accordance with the divine will. Thus the passion narrative is seen as the climax of Jesus' ministry.

**14, 1:** *The Passover and the Feast of Unleavened Bread:* the connection between the two festivals is reflected in Ex 12, 3–20; 34, 18; Lv 23, 4–8; Nm 9, 2–14; 28, 16–17; Dt 16, 1–8. The Passover commemorates the redemption from slavery and the departure of the Israelites from Egypt by night. It began at sundown after the Passover lamb was sacrificed in the temple in the afternoon of the fourteenth day of the month of Nisan. With the Passover Supper on the same evening was associated the eating of unleavened bread. The latter was continued through Nisan 21, a reminder of the affliction of the Israelites and of the haste surrounding their departure. Praise and thanks to God for his goodness in the past were combined at this dual festival with the hope of future salvation. *The chief priests . . . to death:* the intent to put Jesus to death was plotted for a long time but delayed for fear of the crowd (3, 6; 11, 18; 12, 12).

**14, 3–9:** At Bethany on the Mount of Olives, a few miles from Jerusalem, *in the house of Simon the leper,* Jesus defends a woman's loving action of anointing his head with perfumed oil in view of his impending death and burial as a criminal, in which case his body would not be anointed. See further the note on Jn 12, 7. He assures the woman of the remembrance of her deed in the worldwide preaching of the good news.

**14, 12:** *The first day of the Feast of Unleavened Bread . . . the Passover lamb:* a less precise designation of the day for sacrificing the Passover lamb as evidenced by some rabbinical literature. For a more exact designation, see the note on 14, 1. It was actually Nisan 14.

**14, 13:** *A man . . . carrying a jar of water:* perhaps a prearranged signal, for only women ordinarily carried water in jars. The Greek word used here, however, implies simply a person and not necessarily a male.

**14, 18:** *One of you will betray me, one who is eating with me:* contrasts the intimacy of table fellowship at the Passover meal with the treachery of the traitor; cf Ps 41, 10.

**14, 21:** *The Son of Man indeed goes, as it is written of him:* a reference to Ps 41, 10 cited by Jesus concerning Judas at the Last Supper; cf Jn 13, 18–19.

**14, 22–24:** The actions and words of Jesus express within the framework of the Passover meal and the transition to a new covenant the sacrifice of himself through the offering of his body and blood in anticipation of his passion and death. His *blood of the covenant* both alludes to the ancient rite of Ex 24, 4–8 and indicates the new community that the sacrifice of Jesus will bring into being (Mt 26, 26–28; Lk 22, 19–20; 1 Cor 11, 23–25).

**14, 24:** *Which will be shed:* see the note on Mt 26, 27–28. *For many:* the Greek preposition *hyper* is a different one from that at Mt 26, 28 but the same as that found at Lk 22, 19.20 and 1 Cor 11, 24. The sense of both words is vicarious, and it is difficult in Hellenistic Greek to distinguish between them. For *many* in the sense of "all," see the note on Mt 20, 28.

**14, 26:** *After singing a hymn:* Pss 114–118, thanksgiving songs concluding the Passover meal.

**14, 27–31:** Jesus predicted that the Twelve would waver in their faith, even abandon him, despite their protestations to the contrary. Yet he reassured them that after his resurrection he would regather them in Galilee (16, 7; cf Mt 26, 32; 28, 7.10.16; Jn 21), where he first summoned them to be his followers as he began to preach the good news (1, 14–20).

**14, 32–34:** The disciples who had witnessed the raising to life of the daughter of Jairus (5, 37) and the transfiguration of their Master (9, 2) were now invited to witness his degradation and agony and to watch and pray with him.

**14, 36:** *Abba, Father:* an Aramaic term, here also translated by Mark, Jesus' special way of addressing God with filial intimacy. The word ʾ*abbāʾ* seems not to have been used in earlier or contemporaneous Jewish sources to address God without some qualifier. Cf Rom 8, 15; Gal 4, 6 for other occurrences of the Aramaic word in the Greek New Testament. *Not what I will but what you will:* note the complete obedient surrender of the human will of Jesus to the divine will of the Father; cf Jn 4, 34; 8, 29; Rom 5, 19; Phil 2, 8; Heb 5, 8.

**14, 38:** *The spirit is willing but the flesh is weak:* the spirit is drawn to what is good yet found in conflict with the flesh, inclined to sin; cf Ps 51, 7.12. Everyone is faced with this struggle, the full force of which Jesus accepted on our behalf and, through his bitter passion and death, achieved the victory.

**14, 53:** *They led Jesus away . . . came together:* Mark presents a formal assembly of the whole Sanhedrin (chief priests, elders, and scribes) at night, leading to the condemnation of Jesus (64), in contrast to Lk 22, 66.71, where Jesus is condemned in a daytime meeting of the council; see also Jn 18, 13.19–24.

**14, 57–58:** See the notes on Mt 26, 60–61 and Jn 2, 19.

**14, 61–62:** *The Blessed One:* a surrogate for the divine name, which Jews did not pronounce. *I am:* indicates Jesus' acknowledgment that he is the Messiah and Son of God; cf 1, 1. Contrast Mt 26, 64 and Lk 22, 67–70, in which Jesus leaves his interrogators to answer their own question. *You will see the Son of Man . . . with the clouds of heaven:* an allusion to Dn 7, 13 and Ps 110, 1, portending the enthronement of Jesus as judge in the transcendent glory of God's kingdom. *The Power:* another surrogate for the name of God.

**14, 68:** *[Then the cock crowed]:* found in most manuscripts, perhaps in view of vv 30 and 72, but omitted in others.

### *Chapter Fifteen References

| | | | |
|---|---|---|---|
| 15, 1–5: | Mt 27, 1–2.11–14; Lk 23, 1–3. | 24: | Ps 22, 18. |
| 1: | Jn 18, 28. | 27: | Lk 23, 33. |
| 6–15: | Mt 27, 15–26; Lk 23, 17–25; Jn 18, 39–40. | 29: | Jn 2, 19. |
| | | 32: | Lk 23, 39. |
| | | 34: | Ps 22, 2. |
| | | 39–41: | Mt 27, 54–56; Lk 23, 47–49. |
| 16–20: | Mt 27, 27–31; Jn 19, 2–3. | 40: | 6, 3; Lk 8, 2–3. |
| 21: | Mt 27, 32; Lk 23, 26. | 42–47: | Mt 27, 57–61; Lk 23, 50–56; Jn 19, 38–42. |
| 22–38: | Mt 27, 33–51; Lk 23, 32–46; Jn 19, 17–30. | | |

### †Chapter Fifteen Footnotes

**15, 1:** *Held a council:* the verb here, *poieō,* can mean either "convene a council" or "take counsel." This reading is preferred to a variant "reached a decision" (cf 3, 6), which 14, 64 describes as having happened at the night trial; see the note on Mt 27, 1–2. *Handed him over to Pilate:* lacking authority to execute their sentence of condemnation (14, 64), the Sanhedrin had recourse to Pilate to have Jesus tried and put to death (15); cf Jn 18, 31.

**15, 2:** *The king of the Jews:* in the accounts of the evangelists a certain irony surrounds the use of this title as an accusation against Jesus (see the note on 15, 26). While Pilate uses this term (2.9.12), he is aware of the evil motivation of the chief priests who handed Jesus over for trial and condemnation (10; Lk 23, 14–16.20; Mt 27, 18.24; Jn 18, 38; 19, 4.6.12).

**15, 6–15:** See the note on Mt 27, 15–26.

**15, 7:** *Barabbas:* see the note on Mt 27, 16–17.

**15, 13:** *Crucify him:* see the note on Mt 27, 22.

**15, 15:** See the note on Mt 27, 26.

**15, 16:** *Praetorium:* see the note on Mt 27, 27.

**15, 21:** *They pressed into service . . . Simon, a Cyrenian:* a condemned person was constrained to bear his own instrument of torture, at least the crossbeam. The precise naming of Simon and his sons is probably due to their being known among early Christian believers to whom Mark addressed his gospel. See also the notes on Mt 27, 32 and Lk 23, 26–32.

**15, 24:** See the notes on Mt 27, 35 and Jn 19, 23–25a.

**15, 25:** *It was nine o'clock in the morning:* literally, "the third hour," thus between 9 a.m. and 12 noon. Cf vv 33.34.42 for Mark's chronological sequence, which may reflect liturgical or catechetical considerations rather than the precise historical sequence of events; contrast the different chronologies in the other gospels, especially Jn 19, 14.

**15, 26:** *The inscription . . . the King of the Jews:* the political reason for the death penalty falsely charged by the enemies of Jesus. See further the notes on Mt 27, 37 and Jn 19, 19.

**15, 28:** This verse, "And the scripture was fulfilled that says, 'And he was counted among the wicked,' " is omitted in the earliest and best manuscripts. It contains a citation from Is 53, 12, and was probably introduced from Lk 22, 37.

**15, 29:** See the note on Mt 27, 39–40.

**15, 34:** An Aramaic rendering of Ps 22, 2. See also the note on Mt 27, 46.

**15, 35:** *Elijah:* a verbal link with *Eloi* (34). See the note on 9, 9–13; cf Mal 3, 23–24. See also the note on Mt 27, 47.

**15, 38:** See the note on Mt 27, 51–53.

**15, 39:** The closing portion of Mark's gospel returns to the theme of its beginning in the Gentile centurion's climactic declaration of belief that Jesus *was the Son of God.* It indicates the fulfillment of the good news announced in the prologue (1, 1) and may be regarded as the firstfruit of the passion and death of Jesus.

**15, 40–41:** See the note on Mt 27, 55–56.

**15, 43:** *Joseph of Arimathea:* see the note on Mt 27, 57–61.

### *Chapter Sixteen References

| | | | |
|---|---|---|---|
| 16, 1–8: | Mt 28, 1–8; Lk 24, 1–10; Jn 20, 1–10. | 12–14: | Lk 24, 13–35. |
| | | 14: | Lk 24, 36–49; 1 Cor 15, 5. |
| 1–2: | Mt 28, 1; Lk 23, 56. | 15–16: | 13, 10; Mt 28, 18–20; Lk 24, 47; Jn 20, 21. |
| 5: | Jn 20, 12. | | |
| 7: | 14, 28. | 18: | Mt 10, 1; Lk 10, 19; Acts 28, 3–6. |
| 9–20: | Mt 28, 1–10; Jn 20, 11–18. | 19: | Lk 24, 50–53. |
| 10–11: | Lk 24, 10–11; Jn 20, 18. | 20: | 1 Tm 3, 16. |

### †Chapter Sixteen Footnotes

**16, 1–8:** The purpose of this narrative is to show that the tomb is empty and that Jesus *has been raised* (6) and *is going before you to Galilee* (7) in fulfillment of 14, 28. The women find the tomb empty, and an angel stationed there announces to them what has happened. They are told to proclaim the news to Peter and the disciples in order to prepare them for a reunion with him. Mark's composition of the gospel ends at v 8 with the women telling no one, because they were afraid. This abrupt termination causes some to believe that the original ending of this gospel may have been lost. See the following note.

**16, 9–20:** This passage, termed the Longer Ending to the Marcan gospel by comparison with a much briefer conclusion found in some less important manuscripts, has traditionally been accepted as a canonical part of the gospel and was defined as such by the Council of Trent. Early citations of it by the Fathers indicate that it was composed by the second century, although vocabulary and style indicate that it was written by someone other than Mark. It is a general resume of the material concerning the appearances of the risen Jesus, reflecting, in particular, traditions found in Luke (24) and John (20).

The Shorter Ending: Found after v 8 before the Longer Ending in four seventh-to-ninth-century Greek manuscripts as well as in one Old Latin version, where it appears alone without the Longer Ending.

The Freer Logion: Found after v 14 in a fourth-fifth century manuscript preserved in the Freer Gallery of Art, Washington, DC, this ending was known to Jerome in the fourth century. It reads: "And they excused themselves, saying, 'This age of lawlessness and unbelief is under Satan, who does not allow the truth and power of God to prevail over the unclean things dominated by the spirits [*or,* does not allow the unclean things dominated by the spirits to grasp the truth and power of God]. Therefore reveal your righteousness now.' They spoke to

Christ. And Christ responded to them, 'The limit of the years of Satan's power is completed, but other terrible things draw near. And for those who sinned I was handed over to death, that they might return to the truth and no longer sin, in order that they might inherit the spiritual and incorruptible heavenly glory of righteousness. But . . . .' "